Ronald Reagan

Political Quiz Book

By Jay Borland and Malcolm Vance

Exeter Books

NEW YORK

Produced and Packaged: David M. Cohn Publishing, Inc.
Graphics: A Good Thing, Inc.
Jacket Design: Beverly Haw
Composition: Sandcastle
Editorial and Production Services: Cobb-Dunlop, Inc.

Acknowledgements

Dedicated to Roberta Healey Gobin and Joe and Madeline Borland

The authors' special thanks to the following friends who helped along the way (in alphabetical order, so they will remain friends): Judie Annino, Dorothy Chowinski, Dolores Elliott, Hal Haskell, Noreen Kremer, Rhoda Lamson, George Modesta, Rose Sardow, and last, but hardly least, Lewis Chambers, our agent.

PHOTO CREDITS: FROM THE COLLECTION OF THE AUTHOR: p.15; p.25; p.42; p.103(both); p.105; p.113(all). FROM NEWSWEEK: p.33(all); p.41; p.45; p.47; p.77(top); p.83. FROM PENGUIN PHOTOS: p.6; p.9; p.11; p.13. FROM UNITED PRESS INTERNATIONAL: p.17; p.20(all); p.23(both); p.27; p.39; p.50; p.53; p.55; p.57; p.59; p.66; p.68; p.69; p.70; p.72(both); p.77(bottom); p.79(top) Michael Evans(bottom); p.90; p.101.

Contents

Introduction

No one else has ever trod a road to the White House remotely similar to the one that led Ronald Reagan there. If, prior to the autumn of 1980, a Hollywood screenwriter had sumbitted a script about a sports announcer who became a movie star, a movie star who became a six-term president of the Screen Actors Guild, a staunch liberal who became a conservative, a good union man who became the chief spokesperson for General Electric, an affable actor who became a two-term governor of California and an aging, erstwhile thespian who became the President of the United States by an electoral landslide in perhaps the most perilous time in the nation's history, the story would undoubtedly have been dismissed as too far-fetched, too fantastic to be believed!

While truth may not be stranger than all forms of fiction, the true story of Ronald Reagan is certainly more remarkable than the fiction that most editors have permitted to be published or that most producers have allowed to appear on the silver screen. As fiction, it would have defied credulity. As fact, the life of Ronald Reagan is perhaps the most unusual success story in the annals of American history. Paradoxes abound in his rise to the U.S. presidency. The most conservative president in over fifty years, he is also the first to be a proud, card-carrying member of an important union, indeed the former head of (what is now) an AFL/CIO affiliate.

The first divorced President of the United States and a former film star who has remained loyal to Hollywood friends such as Frank Sinatra and Dean Martin, Ronald Reagan was elected with the help of the so-called Moral Majority.

The oldest elected president, who assumed office at an age commensurate to the life expectancy of the average American male, he was shot in the chest and suffered a collapsed lung, but quickly recovered, revealing that he had the constitution of a much younger man and the good-humored courage of the all-American types that he had portrayed on film decades before.

Whatever one's political beliefs (and those of the authors are not necessarily those of Ronald Reagan's), it is impossible not to like and admire the fortieth President of the United States. The man has style. He has wit. He has courage to spare. And most appealing of all, he possesses two traits infrequently found in tandem: rock-ribbed character and abundant charm. Certainly he has led a charmed life. Having gotten into the movies by accident, by simply being-in-the-right-place-at-the-right-time, he went on to become the first President of the United States to recover from a bullet wound while in office. We hope for his sake and the sake of this land that we dearly love, its terrible internal violence notwithstanding, that President Reagan continues to lead a charmed life!

Ronald Reagan and his mother at Warner Bros. Studio during filming of *Stallion Road,* 1947.

RONALD REAGAN'S ROOTS QUIZ

(Score five points for each correct answer.)

1. Ronald Reagan is an American, born and bred. But like everyone in this country, including even American Indians, his ancestors came from elsewhere. What country did Ronald Reagan's paternal grandfather come from originally?

2. According to Ronald Reagan's brother, Neil, the family genealogist, from what catastrophe was their grandfather fleeing in his homeland?

3. Also according to Neil, the grandfather apparently entered the U.S. without proper papers. What would that mean?

4. From what country other than his own did Neil and Ronald's paternal grandfather enter the United States?

5. What was the full name of Ronald Reagan's father?

6. What was the maiden name of Ronald Reagan's mother?

7. Ronald Reagan's mother had a dual (if rather related) ethnic heritage. What two countries did her ancestors come from?

8. To what religion did Ronald Reagan's father belong?

9. To what religion did Ronald Reagan's mother belong?

10. Was Ronald Reagan raised in the religion of his father or his mother?

11. Is Ree-gan or Ray-gan the correct pronunciation of the family name?

12. Ronald Reagan was born on February 6, 102 years after Abraham Lincoln, the first Republican president, was born. In what year was Ronald Reagan born?

13. What is Ronald Reagan's astrological sign?

14. In what town and state was he born?

15. Reagan was born in a two-story brick building. His family had an apartment on the second floor. A retail establishment, whence emanated enticing odors, was on the first floor. What type of store was it?

16. Although the building has now been turned into a mini-museum in this tiny town of about a thousand people, there is still a business establishment on the first floor. A different one, however, than in Ronald's day. What type of business is conducted there now?

RONALD REAGAN'S BOYHOOD QUIZ

(Score five points for each correct answer.)

1. In what Illinois town did the Reagans settle when Ronald was nine years old?
2. It was in this town that Ronald came to young manhood. What river runs through it?
3. What was his father's occupation?
4. What sort of problem did his father suffer from?
5. What high school did Ronald Reagan attend?
6. Ronald Reagan has said, "Our family didn't exactly come from the wrong side of the tracks, but we were certainly always within sound of the ..." Within sound of what?
7. Ronald Reagan's father was a fervent advocate of what political party?
8. What film did Reagan's father not allow his family to see because of its sympathetic portrayal of the Klu Klux Klan?
9. Reagan's father once refused to stay in a hotel because it would not admit people of a certain religious persuasion. What people?
10. Ronald Reagan's mother was a fundamentalist. True or False?
11. Which of his parents instilled in him a love of literature and the dramatic arts?
12. Was Ronald Reagan a poor, average or above average student in high school?
13. Although young Ronald once worked on a construction job, what was his primary summer occupation?
14. How many years did he hold this job?
15. What is the significance of the number 77 in regard to this job?
16. His summer job was on the same river that flowed through town. What was the name of the summer resort where he worked on this job?
17. Young Ronald was always very athletic despite a certain physical defect that ruled out a sport like baseball and years later made him ineligible for combat duty in World War II. What was and is this physical defect?

8

18. In what three sports did Ronald Reagan win letters in high school?
19. He was on the staff of what high school publication?
20. Was he ever president of the student body in high school?

Ronald Reagan won varsity letters in swimming, track, basketball and football at Dixon [Illinois] High School.

RONALD REAGAN'S YOUNG MANHOOD QUIZ

(Score five points for each correct answer.)

1. What was the name of the Illinois college that Ronald Reagan entered in 1928?
2. It was a Christian college with a co-educational student body. About how many students did it have?
3. What post vis-a-vis the student body was Reagan elected to in college?
4. Ronald Reagan was on a partial scholarship and worked his way through college, washing dishes, lifeguarding at the pool and coaching sporting events. True or False?
5. Ronald Reagan was quite a football player in college. What was his position?
6. He captained what other team?
7. When the money-strapped college decided to reduce the faculty during Reagan's freshman year, he helped to organize a student...A student what?
8. Was it successful?
9. Reagan's three college passions were football, politics and dramatics. In his junior year he played a Greek shepherd boy in Edna Saint Vincent Millay's Aria da Capo, which was staged in a one-act play contest at a Big-Ten university. Which one?
10. Reagan and five of his fellow peformers were honored and received an award. Did they win first, second or third prize?
11. Reagan graduated from college with a Bachelor of Arts degree in 1932. In what two subjects had he majored?
12. To what big city did Reagan go in the summer after his graduation looking for a radio job?
13. Rejected at every turn, Reagan hitchhiked home. His father suggested that Ronald take the family car and contact all the radio stations in the surrounding area. Ronald landed a job at the very first station he contacted. In what small city in Iowa was the station located?
14. The station's parent company was World of Chiropractic. Can you guess what the station's call letters were?

15. The World of Chiropractic was founded by Colonel B. J. Palmer of the Palmer School of Chiropractic. Palmer is deceased, but his quite elderly widow lives in Florida. What does Ronald Reagan send her every December?

16. The program director at WOC asked Reagan if he was conversant with a certain sport and if he could do a running commentary on an imagined or remembered game. What sport?

17. Reagan became a sports announcer. What was his recompense for broadcasting his first football game?

18. When he officially signed on with WOC, what was Reagan's monthly salary?

19. Reagan later went to a sister-station with the call letters WHO in another Iowa city. What city?

20. When the station became part of the NBC network, Reagan's sports broadcasts were heard from... From where to where?

Ronald Reagan with members of his football team at Eureka College, Eureka, Illinois.

THE RONALD REAGAN POST-WAR QUIZ

(Score five points for each correct answer.)

Not long after America's entry into World War II, the American Federation of Labor pledged that there would be no strikes for the duration. Hollywood was the only place in which that pledge was not kept. Strikes were rife toward the end of the war. They entailed for the most part demands for higher salaries and better working conditions, but there were sinister overtones in the air and an increasing polarization between the political left and right. There was even talk of a Communist take-over. It was to this witches' brew that Ronald Reagan returned. Describing himself as a "rabid union man," he had been a member of SAG since 1937 and was also one of its officers. In the turbulent post-war years, his involvement with SAG grew more intense.

1. SAG is an acronym for what?
2. Speaking of politics, Reagan was then a staunch Democrat. For what U.S. president, whose name he evoked in his 1980 campaign, had Reagan first voted back in 1932?
3. Looking back on the post-war years, Reagan has said that he was a "bleeding heart" and "a hemophilic..." A hemophilic what?
4. In addition to SAG, Reagan was a board member of the American Veterans Committee and the Holly-wood Hollywood Independent Citizens Committee of Arts, Sciences and Professions. Unwittingly, he also became involved with leftist organizations. Becoming cognizant of the situation and disavowing such organizations, he started to campaign against a type of political influence that he felt was becoming pervasive. What type of political influence?
5. In October of 1947, Reagan was called to Washington, D.C., to testify before the HUAC. What did those initials represent?
6. What was the HUAC investigating?
7. Also, in 1947, Reagan was elected president of something. Of what?

8. How many consecutive terms did he serve in that office?
9. Because of the socio-political turmoil in Hollywood, Reagan at one point feared for his life and carried something for protection. What was that?
10. Due in large part to his increasing political involvement, he and Jane Wyman became estranged and were divorced in 1948. Did she oppose his political views or was she just not that interested in politics?

Ronald Reagan with his first wife, Jane Wyman and their two children, Maureen at 5½ years old and Michael, 16 months, relaxing on the terrace of their Hollywood Hills home in 1946.

THE NEW DIRECTIONS FOR RONALD REAGAN QUIZ

(Score five points for each correct answer.)

1. Nancy Davis and Ronald Reagan became man and wife on March 4, 1952. What handsome Hollywood star and close friend of Ronald Reagan was best man?
2. Who was the matron of honor?
3. In what San Fernando Valley church were Nancy and Ronald wed?
4. The Reagan's first child, Patricia Ann, was born in an emergency operation on October 22, 1952. What type of emergency operation?
5. The Reagan's second and last child, Ronald Prescott, was born on May 20, 1958. In what way was his birth similar to his sister's?
6. Although Reagan resigned as SAG president in 1952, he was on the board of directors until reelected president in 1959. He later resigned, believing that his union positon was incompatible with his other job as spokesman for a production company. What production company?
7. In what year did "The General Electric Theatre" go off the air, leaving Reagan without a job?
8. While working as a spokesman for G.E. and hosting "The General Electric Theatre" had he ever acted on any of its TV presentations?
9. Reagan, who had been a life-long Democrat but had become increasingly conservative over the years, finally joined the Republican party. Had he ever voted Republican before actually becoming one?
10. In 1964 Reagan became the host of another TV series, this one devoted to entertaining and often educational stories about the Old West. What was the name of the series?
11. Who was the sponsor?
12. Also, in 1964, Ronald Reagan made a rousing and subsequently celebrated TV campaign speech for a Republican presidential candidate. Who?
13. Who was his running mate?
14. Who was elected president of the U.S. that year?
15. Who was his running mate?

16. What Hollywood song-and-dance man did Reagan support in his successful bid for the U.S. Senate?

17. In 1965 a group called the Friends of Ronald Reagan urged him to run for governor of California. Of what type of people was this group composed?

18. Also, in 1965, Ronald Reagan published his autobiography, <u>Where's the Rest of Me?</u> What was the source of his title?

19. What job did Reagan give up in 1966 to run for governor?

20. Who was the governor of California at the time that Ronald Reagan decided to run for that job?

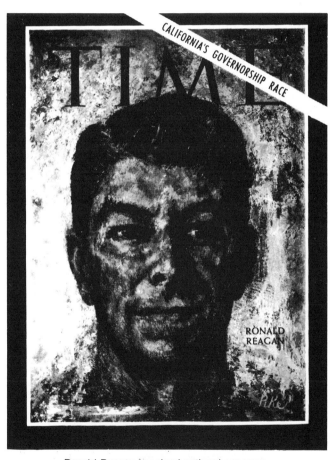

Ronald Reagan received national exposure during the 1966 California gubernatorial race via this *Time* magazine cover story.

THE RONALD REAGAN GUBERNATORIAL QUIZ I

(Score five points for each correct answer.)

1. When a former employer of Ronald Reagan's at a major studio was informed of the actor's guvernatorial ambitions, the movie mogul protested, "No, Jimmy Stewart for Governor. Ronald Reagan as Best Friend." Who was the movie mogul?

2. One very useful thing that Ronald Reagan had in his favor when he entered the political arena was the "recognition factor." What's that?

3. Before Reagan could directly compete for the governorship, he had to win the Republican primary. And he won big, defeating George Christopher, former San Francisco mayor, with 64 percent of the Republican votes. In the Democratic primary, incumbent Pat Brown defeated the nationally known Los Angeles mayor, a controversial and colorful character. Who was he?

4. The race between Ronald Reagan and Governor Brown was heated and occasionally nasty. Brown pointed out to a little black girl in a television commercial that John Wilkes Booth, the man who killed Lincoln, was...A what?

5. Ronald Reagan knew that he had to win an uphill fight. Did registered Democrats outnumber Republicans by a ratio of two-to-one, three-to-two or five-to-three?

6. Reagan had a formidable opponent in Pat Brown, who had been governor since 1958 when he defeated Senate Republican Leader William F. Knowland. Whom had Brown defeated in 1962?

7. It was a wonder that anyone wanted the job. With 19 million people in 1966 and more pouring in every day, California was suffering from an explosion. What kind of explosion?

8. Was California the most heavily populated state in the Union by that time?

9. Only five nations on earth had a greater gross income than the state of California in 1966. One, of course, was the United States. What were the other four nations?

10. What famed comedian called the contest between Brown and Reagan "How the West Was Won"?
11. Reagan accused Brown of being too far left and charged him with a "morality gap" in the state capital. Where was (and still is) the state capital?
12. Brown charged Reagan with being a right-wing extremist and some of Brown's more rabid backers retouched Reagan photographs, giving him a forelock and a toothbrush mustache, making him look like...Whom did they make him look like?
13. Some of Reagan's more embittered backers responded in kind with acerbic bumper stickers that read, "If It's＿＿＿, Flush It." What did the bumper stickers say?
14. How old was Ronald Reagan when he first ran for the governorship of California?
15. How old was Pat Brown at the time?
16. The Democrats employed some of Reagan's fellow thespians to make TV and radio speeches against his candidacy. One Irish-American actor/dancer said, "I've played many roles before the cameras. I've been a soldier, a gambler and even a major league baseball player. I know I could <u>play</u> the role of a governor, but that I could never really sit in his chair and make decisions affecting the education of millions of children." Who made this TV commercial?

Governor Reagan is surrounded by newsmen and pickets as he toured a migrant labor · housing center in Fresno County. Many of the predominately Mexican-American pickets urged the governor to "Go Back to Hollywood".

RONALD REAGAN GUBERNATORIAL QUIZ II

(Score five points for each correct answer.)

In response to the charge of the Democratic opposition that Ronald Reagan was naught but a simple actor who could scarcely speak unless he memorized lines written by others, his staff pointed out that Reagan wrote virtually all of his own speeches. Which, indeed, was true, though most of them were variations on a single stump-speech that he had honed and refined over the years to a polished folksy perfection.

1. It is well-known that to this day Reagan records his speeches on cards that are four-by-six and...What other size?

2. Much to Pat Brown's and the Democratic camp's consternation, Reagan proved to be an exceedingly able campaigner, with a firm grasp on the important political issues.
   "The state constitution says that you have to be a resident for five years in order to run for Governor," observed Reagan. "But you have to be here only 24 hours to get on..." To get on what?

3. There's no suspense as to the outcome of the 1966 gubernatorial contest in California. We all know that Reagan won. But did you know that he won by a landslide? It's true. He won by almost...By almost how many votes?

4. What percentage of the total vote did he receive?

5. In what year did he first take office?

6. Ronald Reagan was not the first film actor to be elected governor of a major state. What star of the silent screen and early talking pictures had been elected governor of Connecticut?

7. "It is," as they say, "a small world." Speaking of governors famous for other things, a governor of the New Mexico Territory late in the last century, who was responsible for Billy the Kid's demise, wrote a bestselling novel that was twice made into a motion picture, the second time with an all-star cast of SAG members, a number of whom knew Ronald Reagan. As for Billy the Kid, he was portrayed on the screen

by several actors who knew Ronald Reagan, including his good friend Roy Rogers. Who was the author/governor and what did he write?

8. What was Reagan forced to do after he assumed the governorship because of the huge financial deficit he inherited?

9. One of the earliest controversies of the Reagan administration was the firing of the University of California's president, Clark Kerr. Although the press gave the impression that Reagan fired Kerr, he was actually dismissed by a state board. What board?

10. When Governor Reagan first took office there were almost a hundred men in San Quentin's death row. How many were excecuted during his two terms?

11. What was Governor Reagan's stand on the death penalty?

12. Ronald Reagan does not smoke, but to this day he loves a type of candy or sweet-treat that became a veritable trademark of his Sacramento administration. What type of candy?

13. Governor Reagan took a tough, no-nonsense approach to the student turmoil on a University of California campus located 10 miles from San Francisco. What campus?

14. Reagan won the support, friendship and respect of the president of the state university in San Francisco, a Japanese-American linguistics expert who later became a U.S. senator and once signed a letter to Reagan with the words: "Your favorite Samurai." Who was he?

15. In what year, as California governor, did Ronald Reagan make an unsuccessful bid to become the Republican candidate for the presidency of the United States?

16. What Republican candidate was elected president of the U.S. that year?

17. Who was his running mate?

18. One of Reagan's strong suits as governor was his ability to delegate something. Delegate what?

19. In what year was Ronald Reagan reelected to the governorship of California?

20. In what month of what year did he begin his second term in office?

Governor Ronald Reagan talks with
Vice-President Spiro Agnew and Pennsylvania's
Governor Raymond Shafer during the start of the
1969 Republican Governors Conference. Reagan
was chairman and Shafer was vice-chairman.

Ronald Reagan received a roaring welcome
during the November 3, 1966 ticker tape parade
through the financial district in downtown
San Francisco.

Governor Ronald Reagan helps heavyweight
boxing champion, George Foreman, with his
world title belt after presentation ceremonies in
Reagan's office in 1972.

RONALD REAGAN'S 1976 CAMPAIGN QUIZ I

(Score five points for each correct answer.)

In August of 1974, when Ronald Reagan was on the last lap of his two-term governorship, Richard M. Nixon, faced with the prospect of impeachment, tearfully resigned from the highest office in the land and perhaps the most important position in the world: the presidency of the United States. Done in by the Watergate scandal, which he had attempted to cover up, Nixon fled from office leaving behind him an untainted vice president, Nelson Rockefeller, and the former minority leader of the House, Gerald Ford, whom Nixon had chosen as his successor. When Ford accepted the presidency of the United States, he modestly informed the American people, "I'm a Ford, not a Lincoln." It was impossible to dislike Jerry Ford. Akin to Ronald Reagan, Ford was a big, affable and easygoing man who projected none of the inner turmoil, personal insecurities and burning resentments that had plagued Richard Nixon from the very inception of his political career. America, after being torn apart by the endless war in Vietnam and the Watergate scandal, welcomed the wholesomeness of Jerry Ford, who called it "A Time for Healing," and, indeed, gave that title to his subsequent autobiography. But not long after assuming office, Ford put a new rent in the body politic by pardoning Richard Nixon, thus assuring that the disgraced former president would not have to spend any time behind bars. Even so, the American people went on liking Jerry Ford. A fairly moderate or middle-of-the-road Republican, he seemed a proverbial shoo-in for that party's presidential nomination in 1976. As it turned out, however, his candidacy was hotly contested by Ronald Reagan.

1. There are moments in a nation's history when the people become aware that only a sharp change of course will solve the problems besetting them," said Ronald Reagan in the National Press Club on November 20, 1975, announcing his candidacy for the presidency of the United States. "We are in such a moment." Where is the National Press Club?

2. As someone who had always prided himself on being a party unifier as opposed to a party divider, Ronald Reagan had hesitated before deciding to wage a primary campaign against an incumbent Republican president, even an appointed one such as Gerald R. Ford. Reagan had long been loath to break the Republican party's eleventh commandment (which some believe he coined). What is the Republican party's "eleventh commandment"?

3. The year 1976 was very special in the history of the American republic. Why?

4. Reagan lost to Ford in the first Republican primary. In what state was it held?

5. Reagan then lost to Ford in three more primaries before the primary in Illinois, which was particularly important because of that state's large number of delegate votes. How did Reagan do in the Illinois primary?

6. After the Illinois primary, Reagan went on the offensive, accusing President Ford of being soft on an economic problem which had prompted Ford to encourage the wearing of WIN buttons. What economic problem?

7. What was Jerry Ford's WIN button an acronym for?

8. Charging that the Ford administration had added $95 billion to the national debt in the past 12 months, Reagan vehemently attacked Big Government... Big Government what?

9. Reagan's most pointed assaults were in the field of foreign policy. He was especially vociferous in his attacks on Ford's secretary of state. Who was Ford's secretary of state?

10. In the Texas primary, Reagan attacked the Ford administration's willingness to relinquish American domination of the U.S.-built "big ditch" in Central America. What was Reagan referring to?

11. How did Reagan fare in the Texas primary?

12. Reagan upset Ford in the Indiana primary, winning 51 percent to 49 percent and taking 45 delegates to Ford's 9. At the University of Notre Dame, Reagan was greeted with red, white and blue banners that read "Welcome Back ___." What was the third word?

13. What type of helmet was Reagan given at Notre Dame?

14. As expected, Reagan won the Georgia primary. How many of Georgia's 48 delegates did he capture?

15. In Alabama, George Wallace's home state, where Reagan captured all 37 delegates, he was aided by the fact that cross-over voting was permitted in the primaries. What is cross-over voting?

Presidential candidate Ronald Reagan shakes hands with senior citizens on the beach in St. Petersburg, Florida.

Presidential hopeful, Ronald Reagan, showing his delight after receiving a birthday cake at the Mt. Sunapee State Park Ski Area, Newbury, N.H. on February 5, 1976—one day before his 65th birthday.

RONALD REAGAN'S 1976 CAMPAIGN QUIZ II

(Score five points for each correct answer.)

1. Were most of the uncommitted Republican delegates thought to support Ford or Reagan?
2. How many delegates are needed to nominate a Republican presidential candidate?

Meanwhile, of course, the Democrats were waging their own primaries. By early May 1976, James Earl Carter, a grinning peanut farmer and former Georgia governor, had pulled ahead of the pack in the Democratic race for delegates. Can you match the delegate numbers on the right to the names and the slots on the left?

3. Carter   A. 193

4. Jackson   B.   80

5. Wallace   C. 144

6. Udall   D.1,818

7. Others   E. 1,190

8. Uncommitted   F. 559

9. Total to Date   G. 232

10. Yet to Be Chosen H. 610

11. How many delegates are needed to nominate a Democratic presidential candidate?
12. Worry was growing in the Republican ranks that if Reagan were nominated the party would suffer a debacle similar to the one in 1964. What staunch Republican said that if Reagan proposes war over the Panama Canal, "he's going to defeat himself"?
13. Many Republicans feared the prospect of a deadlocked convention, whence a dark-horse candidate might emerge. One possible "dark horse" was a tall, handsome, silver-haired former Texas governor. Who was he?
14. Many Republicans were opposed to the tall Texan, however, because he had once been a ...Been a what?
15. In what city in what state did the Republicans hold their 1976 convention?

16. In what convention hall was it held?
17. In what month was it held?
18. In what city did the Democrats hold their 1976 convention?
19. In what convention hall did the Democrats hold their 1976 convention?
20. In what month did the Democrats hold their 1976 convention?

The May 17, 1976 issue of *Time* magazine shows the combatants for the 1976 Republican presidential nomination.

THE 1976 CONVENTION AND ELECTION QUIZ

(Score five points for each answer.)

The tension engendered by the delegate fight at the 1976 Republican Convention was relieved somewhat by the opening-night arrival of the two presidential candidates' radiant wives.

1. Nancy Reagan, arriving first, settled into the glass-enclosed VIP booth high above the north end of the convention floor, wearing a dress of her favorite color. What color is that?

2. Reagan supporters, cheering Nancy as a stand-in for her absent husband, broke into a foot-stamping ovation. Did it go on for more than 5, 10, 15 or 20 minutes?

3. In the midst of the tumult, Mrs. Gerald Ford arrived in an aqua dress and took her seat in the first row above the south end of the convention floor. What was Mrs. Ford's first name?

4. On the second night, Nancy and the Reagan delegates were upstaged by the Ford delegates' thunderous ovation for Betty as the band broke into "Tie a Yellow Ribbon Round the Ole Oak Tree" and she danced briefly with a celebrated singer named Tony. What was his surname?

5. Betty Ford was very critical of Nancy Reagan's opposition to a certain amendment. What amendment?

6. It is customary for presidential nominees to pick their vice-presidential running mates. It was unprecedented for a presidential candidate to pick a running mate. But that was exactly what Ronald Reagan did. Whom did he pick as his running mate?

7. He was a U.S. senator from what state?

8. Was he considered more liberal or about as conservative as Mr. Reagan?

9. In what way did choosing this particular man in such an unprecedented manner hurt Reagan politically?

10. When it came to the delegate roll call for Schweiker's state, his fellow senator proudly announced 93 votes for Jerry Ford. Who was the other senator from Schweiker's state?

11. The role call from what border state that Jimmy Carter would carry in the 1980 election finally pushed Gerald Ford over the 1,130 delegate votes needed for a Republican nomination?
12. Whom did Gerald Ford, eschewing Rockefeller, pick as his 1976 vice-presidential running mate?
13. Ford's running mate was a U.S. senator from what state?
14. What national periodical proclaimed after the Republican convention that "no matter how rosily Reagan looked to his own future, he was finished as a large political power in the country"?
15. Jimmy Carter, of course, received the presidential nod from the Democratic party. Whom did he pick as his vice-presidential running mate?
16. Jimmy Carter's running mate was a U.S. senator from what state?
17. What former Democratic vice-president had been Carter's running mate's political mentor?
18. What was the title of Jimmy Carter's autobiography?
19. What did he promise the American people he would never do to them?
20. Jimmy Carter won the 1976 election. In what month of what year was he inaugurated as president of the United States?

The winner of the 1976 Republican presidential nomination, President Gerald Ford, Vice-President Nelson Rockefeller, and Susan Ford listen to the loser, Ronald Reagan.

THE RONALD REAGAN INTERREGNUM QUIZ

(Score five points for each correct answer.)

An "interregnum" is the interval between two successive regimes or a pause in continuity and refers here to the time that Ronald Reagan spent out of office. After governing California from 1967 to 1975 and then running unsuccessfully for the Republican presidential nomination in 1976, Ronald Reagan spent several years in the political wilderness, licking his wounds and preparing himself for another assault on the presidency.

1. Many people imagined that Ronald Reagan was a relic of the past, that his time had come and gone and that by 1980 it would be too late for him to seek the presidency because of his...His what?

2. There were those who felt that Reagan's 1976 candidacy and (what they perceived as) his lukewarm support for Gerald Ford after the Republican convention cost Ford the election. True or False?

3. Had Reagan been only lukewarm in his support of Ford after the convention?

4. One of the things contributing to Ford's defeat had undoubtedly been the legacy of Watergate, for which Ford was not responsible although he did pardon Richard Nixon. From what we know of the socio-political forces at work in 1976 and the peculiar appeal of Jimmy Carter at that time, how do you think Reagan might have fared had he been the Republican presidential nominee?

5. What right-wing publisher of the Union Leader, a Manchester, New Hampshire, newspaper, wrote to Reagan after the 1976 election, urging him to consider the formation of a third party?

6. Did Reagan ever seriously consider the formation of a third party?

7. Did he ever believe that the Republican party might just benefit from a name change?

8. After the election, Reagan voiced his disenchantment with a wing of liberal Republicans who took their name from the Wisconsin town in which the Republican party had been founded. What town?

28

9. Reagan insisted that the Republican party had to find a way to appeal to factory workers and the ethnic vote and that it had to rid itself of a certain image. The initials of two components of that image are C.C. and B.B. What do the initials represent?

10. The most important political action that Reagan undertook after the 1976 election was perhaps the creation of his own political action committee. What was the name of this committee?

11. In August of 1978, an unusually handsome Illinois congressman, who was chairman of the American Conservative Union, declared his presidential candidacy. What's his name?

12. Where, apparently, was this Illinois congressman trying to outflank Reagan?

What do you think were the results of a Gallup Poll conducted in the spring of 1979, asking Republicans whom they would prefer as their presidential candidate in 1980? Match the percentage on the right to the names on the left.

13. Former Texas governor John Connally   A. 8%

14. Former California governor Ronald Reagan   B. 31%

15. Former U.S. President Gerald Ford   C. 12%

16. Senator Howard Baker of Tennessee   D. 26%

17. Ronald Reagan was referring to America's relations with what country when he said that Carter's "administration doesn't know the difference between being a diplomat and a doormat"?

18. What former CIA director announced his candidacy for the Republican nomination in early May 1979?

19. When asked about his age vis-a-vis the other Republican contenders, Ronald Reagan replied that he might challenge them all to engage him in a contest that entails arm and shoulder strength and ingenuously added, "I think I'd win!" Perhaps he would have. To what kind of contest was Reagan referring?

20. Not counting Gerald Ford, who didn't seem inclined to run, what two Republican hopefuls did Reagan's strategists regard as the most serious threat to their candidate in the autumn of 1979?

RONALD REAGAN RUNS AGAIN QUIZ I

(Score five points for each correct answer.)

In November of 1979, Ronald Reagan formally announced his third candidacy for the Republican party's presidential nomination in a most unlikely setting for a GOP gathering: a northeastern city which to many conservative, Sunbelt Republicans was the very intersanctum of the enemy.

1. In what city did Reagan announce his candidacy?
2. In what hotel?
3. Was Reagan's speech on national television?
4. To whom did Reagan lose in the Iowa caucuses in January of 1980?

After his defeat in the Iowa caucuses, Reagan knew that he had to do well in the first state primary, in New Hampshire. He had already been in a debate on national TV with six other candidates: two Illinois congressmen, a former Texas governor, a former Texas congressman, a senator from Tennessee and a senator from Kansas.

5. Who were the two House representatives from Illinois?
6. Who was the former Texas governor?
7. Who was the former House representative from Texas?
8. Who was the senator from Tennessee?
9. Who was the senator from Kansas?

A second debate-in which Reagan had challenged Bush to go one-on-one was scheduled for the evening of January 29, 1980, the Saturday night before the crucial New Hampshire primary.

10. The debate was to be sponsored by a Nashua, New Hampshire newspaper. What was the one-word name of the newspaper?
11. Two days before the debate, the Federal Election Commission ruled that the newspaper's sponsorship was tantamount to an illegal campaign contribution.

Reagan suggested to Bush that they split the $3,500 tab. Bush said no. What did Reagan do?

12.   Where in Nashua was the debate to be held?

On the day of the debate, Reagan began to wonder whether or not he should portray Bush as his primary rival. Reagan's aides then invited the other candidates to debate. Not knowing of this Reagan maneuver which was completely legal Bush was surprised when he arrived on the scene. Approaching the dais, he was asked to join the other candidates in the anteroom. Bush declined, contending that he didn't have time.

13.   Who was the only candidate who had appeared in the first debate who didn't appear for this one?
14.   When Reagan and Bush and the other four candidates finally gathered on the dais, the moderator-Joe Breen, editor of the Telegraph insisted that the one-on-one format could not be changed. Reagan angrily grabbed the microphone. Breen then turned the power off and Reagan shouted something. What did he shout?

All hell broke loose. Bush appeared perplexed. "I was invited here by the editors of the Nashua newspaper," he said. "I am their guest. I will play by the rules, and I am glad to be here." This was interpreted as support for the two-man format. Anderson, Dole, Crane and Baker bolted from the dais, fuming and snorting, charging Bush with having silenced them.

15.   Which of the four said, "The responsibility for this whole travesty rests with Mr. Bush"?
16.   The aide to one of the senators in the abortive debate said, "There were cells in Reagan's body that hadn't seen blood in years. He was terrific!" Which senator?

Mr. Bush, who had been trying to convince the New Hampshire voters that he would be "a president we won't have to train," came off with egg on his face. Ronald Reagan, on the other hand, was perceived as being masterful.

17. Not only did Reagan win the New Hampshire primary, he swamped George Bush by more than two-to-one. Indeed, Reagan's win was so big that he won...
  A. more votes than Bush and Baker combined.
  B. more votes than Bush, Baker and Connally combined.
  C. more votes than Bush, Baker, Connally and Anderson combined.
  D. more votes than Bush, Baker, Connally, Anderson and Dole combined.
  E. more votes than Bush, Baker, Connally, Anderson, Dole and Crane combined.

After the early April primaries in Wisconsin, Louisiana and Kansas, President Jimmy Carter and candidate Ronald Reagan were far ahead of all other candidates in their respective parties vis-a-vis the number of delegates they had garnered.

18. What Democratic governor from a western state was forced to drop out of the primary race after his poor showing in Wisconsin?

19. On the Republican side, a third-place showing in Wisconsin ruined a GOP maverick's chances of winning his party's nomination and raised serious doubts about his ability to mount a third-party challenge. Who was he?

20. Although Democratic Senator Ted Kennedy had won surprising victories in the New York and Connecticut primaries, he did poorly in the more conservative Midwest, where voters raised questions about his character. Politically, Kennedy was still haunted by a tragedy that had happened over 10 years before. What tragedy?

The 1980 Republican presidential candidates debate in Nashua, N.H. Included are Connally, Bush, Baker, Anderson, Dole and Crane.

RONALD REAGAN RUNS AGAIN QUIZ II

(Score five points for each correct answer.)

1. Many independent and Democratic voters in Wisconsin, distrustful of Kennedy and disgruntled by Carter, voted Republican in the primary. Did independents and Democrats constitute 10 percent, 25 percent or more than 50 percent of the GOP primary vote?
2. Incidentally, what does GOP stand for?
3. In liberal Wisconsin, Reagan beat his closest competitor by 40 percent to 31 percent. Who was Reagan's closest competitor?
4. In the home state of Bob Dole, Reagan swamped George Bush 63 percent to 13 percent. What state is that?
5. What outspoken, controversial, white-haired Republican received 18 percent of the primary vote in Bob Dole's state?
6. During the 1980 primary campaign, Ronald Reagan occasionally displayed a penchant for putting his foot in his mouth. Whom did he mistakenly claim were "not eligible for GI Bill of Rights benefits with regard to education or anything"?
7. He also felt compelled to explain that his reference to "young bucks" with food stamps in a grocery line was not meant as a slur against...Against whom?
8. What former president did Ronald Reagan erroneously claim had asked for a 30 percent tax cut in 1963?
9. Speaking of tax cuts, what was the name of the 30 percent tax-cut bill that Reagan supported?
10. In the middle of May 1980, Reagan criticized as inhumane attempts by the Carter administration to prevent American boat operators from making unauthorized trips to pick up refugees from a foreign country. What country?
11. In June of 1980, Robert Hughes, Republican chairman in the Cleveland area, observed that white-ethnic, blue-collar workers who tended to be Democrats, but were often very conservative on the social issues liked Reagan's "views on abortion, strong national

defense, tough law and order." But Mr. Hughes also observed that they were "leery" of Ronald Reagan on issues relating to...Relating to what?

On June 14, 1980, at a $500-a-plate Republican fund-raising dinner to pay off campaign debts, George Bush, Howard Baker, John Connally, Philip Crane and Bob Dole acknowledged their defeat by Ronald Reagan and pledged fealty to him. Oh, yes, there was another losing candidate in attendance, Mexican-American businessman Benjamin Fernandez.

12. Of all the candidates, including Reagan, who had the most international experience?
13. Who was the shortest?
14. In what Beverly Hills hotel was the gala event held?

Among those in the audience were Jimmy Stewart, Irene Dunne, Don DeFore, Joseph Cotten and Robert Stack. Entertainment was provided by singers Tanya Tucker and Pat Boone.

15. What actor who had played an FBI man on television was the master of ceremonies?

Five of the men who were in Reagan's inner circle at the time are listed below on the left. Their specialties are listed on the right. Match the specialties on the right to the men on the left.

16. William E. Simon   A. Domestic policy

17. Lyn Nofziger   B. Chief of staff

18. Edwin Meese   C. Communications

19. Martin Anderson   D. National security

20. Richard V. Allen   E. Economics

THE 1980 REPUBLICAN CONVENTION QUIZ I

(Score five points for each correct answer.)

It is easy to be cynical about American political conventions. On one level, they are no more than pre-packaged pep rallies, and as such they can be incredibly boring. At their worst, they seem no more than empty rituals. But even then perhaps especially then there is a poignancy about them, revealing as they do the age-old human urge to make some sense out of life by the observance of rituals, be they artistic, religious or political. To sneer at rituals is to sneer at human need. And the rituals that the Democrats and Republicans hold every four years go to the heart of the American experience and our governmental process. For all the celebrated silliness, occasional sordidness and phony hoopla surrounding American political conventions, there is about them something as touching as a small and trusting child playing with a big and loving dog, something that speaks to our sense of wonder.

1. The first full-blown American political convention took place in the fourth decade of the last century. What was the year?
2. Under the new convention rules drafted after the Democratic debacle of 1968 in Chicago, the results of the primaries are binding on the convention delegates, be they Republican or Democrat. Although uncommitted delegates may still pick a presidential nominee at the convention itself, delegates who have already been won by a presidential nominee in the primaries cannot bolt to someone else. True or False?

There was no suspense as to who would receive the presidential nomination at the 1980 Republican Convention. Ronald Reagan was the aging Crown Prince, awaiting his investiture. But Reagan injected suspense into the proceedings when, desirous of a "dream ticket," he asked Gerald Ford to be his vice-presidential running mate on the convention's second day. Ford didn't say yes, and he didn't say no, keeping Reagan, the conventioneers, the media and the American public in suspense for 36 hours.

3. One of Ford's conditions was his choice of secretary of state. Whom did Ford want for that post?
4. What was Reagan's reaction?
5. Reagan offered to share his presidential powers with Ford. True or False?
6. When Ford finally declined what person close to him was probably greatly relieved?
7. Actually, it might not have been a "dream ticket." Ford, after all, had been the first incumbent U.S. president to suffer defeat since... Since whom?
8. What former presidential candidate who'd had good reason to expect the vice presidential nod from Reagan undoubtedly went through agony until he was chosen after all?
9. In what city did the 1980 Republican Convention take place?
10. In what month?
11. What Afro-American Democrat was the mayor of that city?
12. Did Glen Campbell or Pat Boone lead the Pledge of Allegiance as the convention opened?
13. Did Glen Campbell or Pat Boone sing the national anthem with Tanya Tucker?
14. What religious leader gave the invocation that first evening?
15. After the invocation, the speakers got down to business, castigating President Carter for incredible ineptitude. What conservative economist said, "Surely, this administration will go down in history as the worst stewards of the American economy in our lifetime"?
16. Former President Gerald Ford delivered the most stinging attack on Carter, pointing out quite accurately that the "misery index" on which Carter had assaulted Ford four years before had actually doubled during Carter's administration. What are the two components of the "misery index"?
17. On the convention's second night, the executive director of the NAACP spoke to the assembled. Who was he?
18. What former GOP presidential candidate reminisced about 1964?

THE 1980 REPUBLICAN CONVENTION QUIZ II

(Score five points for each correct answer.)

1. What former secretary of state was the final speaker on the second night?

The third night began with Michigan Congressman Guy Vander Jagt quoting from Thomas Jefferson and Henry Wadsworth Longfellow and reciting in its protracted entirety a poem by a patriotic versifier named Henry Van Dyke. Here's a sample verse...

> I know that Europe's wonderful, yet
> something seems to lack:
> The Past is too much with her, and
> the people looking back.
> But the glory of the Present is to
> make the Future free—
> We love our land for what she is
> and what she is to be.

2. What is the name of the poem?
3. Finally, Ronald Reagan's name was put into nomination by Senator Paul...Paul who?
4. After several people seconded the nomination, the states cast their delegate votes in alphabetical order. The 20 votes of what Big Sky state pushed Reagan over the 998 needed for nomination?
5. Bedlam broke loose as 12,000 red-white-and-blue balloons fell from above and Manny Harmon's Convention Orchestra played a medley of rousing marches. Marches by whom?
6. Surrounded by his wife and four grown children, Reagan watched the proceedings on television in this 69th-floor hotel suite. In what hotel was he staying?
7. After giving Nancy a victory kiss, Reagan drove in a motorcade to the arena where he acknowledged the cheers of the multitude and announced his running mate. In what arena did the Republican Convention take place?
8. The following evening, Reagan officially accepted the nomination and addressed the nation, making

what was probably the best speech thus far in his incredible career, casting an appeal to all Americans regardless of sex, class or color, quoting an 18th-century liberal, "We have it in our power to begin the world all over again." Whom was he quoting?

9. To what was Reagan referring when he said it was "never more dangerous than when our desire to have it help us blinds us to its great power to harm us"?

10. What former Democratic president did Reagan quote on the danger of Big Government?

11. Reagan said it was vital to create new...New what?

12. "For those without skills, we'll find a way to help them get new skills. For those without job opportunities we'll stimulate new opportunities, particularly in..." In where?

13. In lieu of reading from his customary three-by-five or four-by-six cards, Reagan read from what?

14. Did he also have a typewritten copy of his speech?

15. What did Reagan request from the audience at the end of his speech?

16. What were Reagan's last three words?

17. After Reagan's acceptance speech, he was joined on the podium by his vice-presidential running mate. Both men were wearing dark, conservative suits. Reagan's shirt was white. What color was Bush's shirt?

18. Although different in color, their shirts had the same type of cuffs. What type of cuffs?

Republican presidential candidate Ronald Reagan adds some finishing touches to his acceptance speech at his Pacific Palisades home before leaving to attend the Republican Convention in Detroit.

THE 1980 REPUBLICAN CONVENTION QUIZ III

(Score five points for each correct answer.)

1. Was the 1980 gathering in Detroit the 28th, 29th, 30th, 31st, 32nd, 33rd, 34th or 35th Republican Convention?
2. Was the convention composed of 2,500, 3,000, 3,500, 4,000, 4,500 or 5,000 delegates and alternates?
3. At the beginning of his acceptance speech, Ronald Reagan thanked Detroit for its "warm hospitality." The Republicans were unanimous in their praise for the financially beleaguered motor city and Mayor Coleman Young. The GOP chairman said, "I'm getting overwhelming compliments about Detroit. This city has busted its rear." Who was the GOP chairman?
4. How many members of Detroit's 4,800-man police force patrolled the downtown district during the convention?
5. Approximately how many trees and shrubs were planted along Detroit's highways and byways?
6. What type of display, costing $8,000, illuminated the night sky on convention eve?
7. What had Mayor Young managed to settle just three days before the convention?

As for the 32nd Republican Convention itself, it was, of course, an unqualified success. It nominated a contender who went on to win the presidency of the United States. At the time, however, no one knew for certain who would win that office.

8. Although Reagan's polls gave him a 15-point lead over President Carter, that was expected to dwindle after the Democrats did something. Did what?
9. Reagan's strategists urged him to run scared, as if he were an underdog. True or False?
10. Reagan, who had created the 11th Republican commandment ("Thou shalt not speak ill of other Republicans"), began speaking of a 12th commandment. What was it?
11. What Arizona congressman, who was the convention's permanent chairman, said, "Four years ago, we had

the purists against the pragmatists. This year 90 percent of the people here are pragmatists. It's a good omen"?

12. Virtually all the delegates seemed to have a good time despite the terrible heat that put a severe strain on the Joe Louis Arena's...The arena's what?

13. It was ironically fitting that Reagan received the nomination in an arena named after the great "Brown Bomber" as he and Reagan once worked in a film together. True or False?

14. The striped ties and Brooks Brothers suits of the northeastern-style Republicans were far outnumbered on the convention floor by the Sunbelt's polyester suits and buttons that read "Stop..." Stop what?

15. What Democrat from the Midwest, who had helped to write Jack Kennedy's inaugural address, said of Reagan's acceptance speech, he "tried to make the tent he was constructing large enough to hold a significant portion of the population, and I think he did it"?

Republican presidential candidate Ronald Reagan planning economic strategy with advisors Greenspan and Shultze.

Time magazine shows Reagan and Bush enjoying their nomination at the 1980 Republican Convention.

THE GEORGE BUSH QUIZ I

(Score five points for each correct answer.)

1. George Bush is how many years younger than Ronald Reagan?
2. How much older is Bush than his wife?
3. What's her name?
4. What is George Bush's full name?
5. Unlike Reagan, Bush came from an affluent and sophisticated family. Bush's father was a U.S. senator from what eastern state?
6. What was Bush's father's business?
7. George Bush had an excellent education. From what exclusive prep school did he graduate?
8. From what Ivy League college did he graduate?
9. What year did he graduate?
10. Bush's wife came from a similar background. She was the daughter of a wealthy executive in a business devoted to the written word. What was her father's business?
11. Where in New York State did she grow up?
12. From what fashionable girls' school in Charleston, South Carolina, did she graduate?
13. What college did she attend?
14. She dropped out of college to marry George Bush. They met while both were home on vacation. What time of year was it?
15. At what type of function did they meet?
16. In what Texas city did George and Barbara make their home before the 1980 election?
17. In what Texas business did George Bush become a millionaire?
18. George Bush spent 32 years in Texas before the 1980 election. Did it make any appreciable difference in his "preppy" voice, speech and appearance?
19. It is well-known that George Bush was a CIA director. But he also served in Congress from 1967 to 1970. Was he in the House or the Senate?
20. Incidentally, what does CIA stand for?

THE GEORGE BUSH QUIZ II

(Score five points for each correct answer.)

1. George Bush, who is now vice president of the United States, has an incredibly impressive dossier. In addition to being a CIA director and a congressman, he served as a U.S. ambassador. He was not, however, an ambassador to any particular country, but rather to an international organization. What organization?
2. To what Asian country was he an envoy?
3. What was George Bush awarded in World War II for "heroism and extraordinary achievement" as a U.S. Navy fighter pilot?
4. When he was nominated at the Republican Convention, George Bush did not talk at great length, correctly pointing out that "this is Ronald Reagan's night. He is the man whom you and the American people are waiting to hear." How long was Bush's unusually short speech?
5. Although Bush is perceived by some people as being considerably more liberal than Reagan, the truth is that they are almost equally conservative. The primary political difference between them is not so much in substance, but in...In what?
6. For all of Bush's basic conservatism, he was somewhat suspect among Sunbelt Republicans. How do you explain that?
7. What commission of which George Bush was a member was suspect among Sunbelt Republicans?
8. Speaking of the Sunbelt, a number of Americans have migrated to that region in recent years from...From what section of the country?
9. What right-wing New Hampshire publisher disparparagingly referred to George Bush as a "clean-fingernails Republican"?
10. Given Reagan's and Bush's political backgrounds, in what policy area should George Bush be most helpful to Ronald Reagan?
11. What group of people close to Ronald Reagan favored George Bush as the vice-presidential candidate if Gerald Ford wasn't available?

12. Nancy Reagan particularly liked George Bush and strongly urged her husband to pick him. True or False?

13. At one point Reagan questioned whether or not Bush was tough enough. True or False?

14. Bush and Reagan campaigned against each other in the primaries and naturally had their differences. What proposal of Reagan's did Bush call "voodoo economics" and "pie in the sky"?

15. What three-word amendment opposed by both Reagan and the Republican platform did Bush support?

16. Bush was opposed to the implementation of a constitutional amendment banning something. Banning what?

17. In how many primaries did Bush beat Ronald Reagan?

18. Three exceedingly important states in which Bush beat Reagan during the primaries were Michigan, Massachusetts and the state from which Reagan had drawn his vice-presidential running-mate-to-be (but never was) in 1976. What state is that?

19. Perhaps to point out how much younger he was than Ronald Reagan, during the primaries Bush kept bragging that he did something two to three miles every day. Did what?

20. When Reagan suggested that the U.S. blockade Cuba in response to the Soviet invasion of Afghanistan, Bush pointed out "the Cubans didn't invade Afghanistan. The Soviets did." He also noted that a blockade of Cuba would tie up something. Tie up what?

George Bush makes his point during the New Hampshire Republican presidential debate.

THE JOHN ANDERSON QUIZ

(Score five points for each correct answer.)

During the Detroit convention, the GOP's prodigal son, John Anderson, who had already declared himself an independent presidential candidate, was off on a whirlwind tour of the Old World, visiting five nations in a dozen days.

1. His first stop was Israel. Where did he pray there in public?
2. He met the Israeli Prime Minister. Who was that?
3. Did Anderson support or oppose President Carter's view that Israeli settlements along the Arab-occupied West Bank were "an obstacle to peace"?
4. Anderson advocated the Israeli annexation of the Arab section of a certain city. What city?
5. What noted Egyptian leader with whom Anderson met dubbed him "the George Washington of the Middle East"?
6. Anderson took what he called "a sentimental journey" to a German city where he had met his wife while stationed there as a Foreign Service officer. What German city?
7. What was Anderson's wife's first name?
8. In Bonn, he talked with the West German chancellor. Who was that?
9. Why did they meet in Bonn as opposed to another West German city?
10. In Paris, the French president refused to grant Anderson an audience. Who was the French president?
11. Anderson did meet, however, with Raymond Barre. What was his position in the French government?
12. In England, Anderson received a warm reception from the British prime minister. Who was that?
13. The prime minister and presidential candidate Anderson got along famously, and she invited him to hold an impromptu press conference on the very doorstep of her address. What was her address?
14. Referring to the convention in Detroit, Anderson commented that Bush "had to accept a platform that

puts the Republican party outside the..." Outside the what?

15. When Bush evoked the name of Adlai Stevenson, the twice-defeated Democratic nominee beloved by the British, a reporter inquired, "What makes you think you can win the presidency on the basis of intelligence and realism if Adlai Stevenson could not?" Anderson replied: "I am not running against..." Whom did he say he was not running against?

16. Anderson was a congressman from what state?

17. Why did the fairly liberal stance taken by Anderson in his presidential campaign meet with skepticism in some quarters?

18. What did Anderson have in common with both Carter and Reagan in regard to religion?

19. When Anderson first went to Congress in the early 1960s he wanted to make Christianity the state religion of the U.S. True or False?

20. Anderson has the same color hair as George Bush's wife. What color is that?

John Anderson joins his "fellow" Republicans in the debate in New Hampshire.

THE MORAL MAJORITY QUIZ

(Score five points for each correct answer.)

One very curious fact about the 1980 presidential campaign was that all three major candidates-Reagan, Carter and Anderson were born-again Christians. The members of the Moral Majority, a right-wing evangelical movement that endorsed Reagan, might be surprised to learn, if they are not already aware, that many of America's Founding Fathers were deists, who believed that while God created the world and set it in motion, much as a watchmaker creates a fine timepiece, He did not intervene in its affairs after that. And when the Founding Fathers drafted the Constitution and the Bill of Rights, they insisted on a strict separation of church and state. Notwithstanding that fact, Americans have long been a religious people. Only four presidents-Jefferson, Lincoln, Andrew Johnson and Rutherford B. Hayes had no formal affiliation with an organized form of religion. Could a Jefferson or a Lincoln be elected today? There is, of course, no way to know for certain. Three U.S. presidents- John Adams, John Quincy Adams and William Howard Taft were members of the Unitarian Church, which does not subscribe to the divinity of Christ. All that is by way of preface to the purpose of this quiz: 20 questions on the Moral Majority's involvement in the 1980 presidential campaign. Incidentally, it is important to keep in mind that not all evangelicals are politically conservative. Some are politically liberal. Perhaps a few are even on the far left. Traditionally, however, evangelicals have been politically apathetic, and in the past many never bothered to register, let alone vote. It was to these people that the Moral Majority tried to appeal in 1980.

1. George Gallup calculated the number evangelicals of of voting age in the U.S. What number did he arrive at?
2. Gallup's number represented what percent of America's adult population?
3. Who founded the Moral Majority movement in June of 1979?

4. What Virginia city is his home base?
5. What is the name of his gospel-hour TV show that appears on nearly 400 stations?
6. The Moral Majority movement is opposed to abortion and the Equal Rights Amendment and undoubtedly influenced the Republican...The Republican what (other than its presidential candidate)?
7. What presidential candidate, himself a born-again Christian, described the wedding of the Moral Majority and the New Right as "a union which seeks to inject unbending rigidity and intolerance into church pew and polling booth alike"?
8. In all fairness, liberal clegymen lobbying for civil rights and opposing the Vietnam War-had been more active politically in recent years than the religious right-wing. Prior to 1980, the last time conservative small town fundamentalists made themselves felt was in 1919 when they persuaded Congress to pass the 18th Amendment to the Constitution. What was the 18th Amendment?
9. Moral Majority members took command of an entire state delegation to the Republican Convention. What state delegation?
10. One of the issues that really fires up the Moral Majority has to do with something that is not allowed in public schools. What is it that Moral Majority members want to see put back into the classrooms?
11. Candidate Reagan received some flack from the press when, speaking to a group of conservative evangelicals in Texas, he questioned the validity of a well-established scientific theory. What theory?
12. When asked in Lynchburg, Virginia, about voluntary prayer in public schools, Reagan said he believed that something should never have been expelled from the classroom. What (other than prayer itself) did he say had been expelled?
13. Although the Moral Majority is the best known of the right-wing evangelical movements, there are others such as the Religious Roundtable, which enourages religious conservatives to go out and vote. By whom was it founded?
14. The Reverend Richard Zone heads a right-wing religious movement which, disclaiming tax-exemption

status, actually campaigns for and against specific political candidates. What is the name of Zone's organization?

15. Was it Zone or Falwell who said: "We can talk about a balanced budget as a moral issue. The Bible says you should not live in debt"?

16. Although right-wing evangelical movements have a predominantly white membership, more blacks than whites are evangelicals on a per capita basis. True or False?

17. In addition to opposing abortion, pornography, the ERA, sex education in the schools and the so-called Godless schools, the Moral Majority is against the death penalty. True or False?

18. What Catholic periodical, published by Jesuits, claimed that the right-wing evangelicals were preaching "moral fascism"?

19. The right-wing evangelicals are resentful of an establishment-church organization with the initials NCC. What do the initials represent?

20. Rabbi Marc Tanenbaum, head of the American Jewish Committee, charged that the right-wing evangelicals were attempting to impose upon public officials a "religious test," one that was forbidden by the United States Constitution. Which article to the Constitution states that "no religious Test shall ever be required as a qualification to any Office or public Trust under the United States"?

During the 1980 presidential campaign, Ronald Reagan and daughter, Maureen, agreed to disagree on many rights issues. Here Maureen hosts TV talk show with her father, outgoing California Governor Reagan, in 1975.

THE WOES OF JIMMY CARTER QUIZ

(Score five points for each correct answer.)

"Man is born unto trouble as the sparks fly upward." Job, Chapter 5, Verse 2

Jimmy Carter, the upward striver from Georgia, the first high school graduate in his family, the man who graduated from Annapolis 59th in a class of 820, the born-again Baptist, the former Georgia governor, the engineer turned successful peanut farmer, the loving father and devoted husband, was clearly a hard working, highly intelligent and well-meaning United States president. So what went wrong? Why did the American people, who admired him as a man, turn against him and choose Ronald Reagan in what was an electoral-if not quite popular-vote landslide?

First, we must ask: "What makes a good president?" Clearly, high intelligence and good character are woefully insufficient by themselves. A good president inspires confidence in his ability to govern. A good president projects a sense of strength and leadership. This Jimmy Carter failed to do. While many of his problems were not of his own making, his response to those problems left the nation with a sense of unease.

Part of Jimmy Carter's problem was his isolation-largely self-imposed from official Washington and Capitol Hill. It has been said that in the final analysis the Carter presidency consisted of six people, all Georgians. Two of them, of course, were Carter himself and his wife, Rosalynn. The other four are listed below on the left. Their positions are listed on the right. Match them.

1. Jody Powell   A. Domestic advisor
2. Charles Kirbo   B. Press secretary
3. Hamilton Jordan   C. Attorney and friend
4. Stuart Eizenstat   D. Political strategist

5. A seemingly poor student of human nature, Jimmy Carter apparently failed to grasp the uses of power. Though he belonged to a religion that emphasized

original sin, he seemed to believe that even the Soviets always told the truth and were well-intentioned. In his dealings with foreign leaders, Jimmy Carter seemed downright naive. Having been assured by the head of the Soviet Union of that country's peaceful intentions, Carter was indignantly surprised when the Soviets invaded a neighboring country in December of 1979. What country did the Soviets invade?

6. Who was Carter's counterpart in the Soviet Union?

7. What was the name of President Carter's personal friend, fellow Georgian and economic adviser who was forced from the Office of Management and Budget due to questions of financial impropriety?

8. Jimmy Carter's brother, Billy, was also an embarrassment. With what Middle Eastern country had Billy tried to make a questionable oil deal?

9. What UN ambassador under Carter was forced to resign when it was revealed that he'd had a secret meeting with the PLO?

10. Of the major Republican candidates whom did Carter think he had the best chance of beating?

11. What was Ronald Reagan's rather clever reply when Jimmy Carter accused him of being "irresponsible"?

On the international scene, Carter's greatest woe and America's severest humiliation was the Iranian crisis. The Shah of Iran, an American ally who had been forced to flee his country, was living in Mexico and dying of cancer in the autumn of 1979. Iran was in a state of chaos, with two factions vying for power: the secular technocrats led by Prime Minister Mehdi Bazargan and the fanatically religious forces led by the Islamic mullahs and the Ayatollah Khomeini, an embittered zealot who hated the modern world and was revered as a Holy Man by millions of his countrymen.

12. When the Shah was admitted into the U.S. for medical treatment, the Ayatollah Khomeini's rabid followers took over their country and the American Embassy in Teheran. Two Americans, a banker and a former secretary of state, had reputedly influenced Carter's decision to admit the Shah. What two Americans?

13. On what date did the Iranian "students" seize the American embassy?

14. On Thanksgiving Day, 1979, the Iranians released 13 American hostages. What distinguished them from most of the remaining hostages?

15. Whom did the Iranians demand in exchange for the remaining hostages?

16. After the Shah left New York City, he went to Texas for a while before going to a Central American country. What country?

17. In what country did the Shah finally die?

18. In the spring of 1980, an abortive military attempt was made to rescue the hostages. It was canceled when an American helicopter collided with a C-130 transport plane in Iran itself. How many American servicemen tragically lost their lives in the fiery fiasco?

19. Cyrus Vance, who had opposed the mission from the very beginning, resigned as secretary of state. Whom did Carter name as Vance's replacement?

20. In June of 1980, the Iranians, probably not wanting a dead hostage on their hands, released Richard Queen, who was suffering from multiple sclerosis. (Fortunately, he recovered.) How many hostages remained in Iran?

President Jimmy Carter kisses his wife, Rosalynn, after the 90 minute presidential debate with Ronald Reagan in Cleveland on October 31, 1980.

THE CARTER/REAGAN DEBATE QUIZ

(Score five points for each correct answer.)

Although the big debate between President Carter and candidate Reagan will probably not go down in history alongside the Lincoln/Douglas debates, it did help to determine the outcome of the 1980 election by disabusing many voters of the Carter-fostered notion that Reagan was a trigger-happy, hip-shooting, right-wing hawk.

1. What was the day of the week and the date on which the great debate took place?
2. In what city did the debate take place?
3. What organization sponsored the debate?
4. What retired commentator for ABC News moderated the debate?
5. The debate had four panelists. Which one was a woman?
6. How long was the debate?
7. After the debate, Ronald Reagan managed to surprise and upstage Jimmy Carter by walking over to him and performing an obligatory ritual. What ritual?

What follows are nine quotes from the debate. It's up to you to recall who said what?

8. "And I happen to believe that we've made great progress from the days when I was young and when this country didn't even know it had a racial problem."
9. "Those who suffered from discrimination because of race or sex certainly knew we had a racial problem."
10. "Ultimately, the most serious terrorist threat is if one of those radical nations who believe in terrorism as a policy should have atomic weapons."
11. "I don't think there's any doubt that in the future the cost of oil is going to go up."
12. "I'm not so sure it means steadily higher fuel costs, but I do believe that this nation has been portrayed for too long a time to the people as being energy poor when it is energy rich."

13. "One of the commitments that I made was to deregulate the major industries of this country."
14. "The American people now are facing, next Tuesday, a lonely decision."
15. "I would like to have a crusade today. And I would like to lead that crusade with your help."
16. "I believe the presidency is what Teddy Roosevelt said it was! It's a bully pulpit."

The three panelists, other than Barbara Walters, are listed below on the left. The periodicals which they represented are listed on the right. Match them.

17. Harry Ellis   A. Editor, <u>U.S. News & World Report</u>

18. William Hillard   B. Reporter, <u>The Christian Science Monitor</u>

19. Marvin Stone   C. Assistant managing editor, <u>The Portland Oregonian</u>

20. Did the debate have an apparent affect on the election's outcome?

President Carter and his Republican challenger, Ronald Reagan, greet each other prior to debate in Cleveland.

THE 1980 ELECTION QUIZ I

(Score five points for each correct answer.)

1. Until the last few days before the election, it was deemed "too close to call" by most of the pollsters. True or False?
2. Ronald Reagan's big win was not quite the overwhelming landslide that the electoral vote would lead us to believe. He beat Carter by only 10 percent of the popular vote. What percentage of the popular vote did Reagan and Carter receive?
3. Within one million, how many popular votes did Reagan receive?
4. Within one million, how many popular votes did Carter receive?
5. Within one million, how many popular votes did Anderson receive?
6. To get back to the electoral votes, how many are needed to win a presidential election?
7. How many electoral votes did Reagan receive?
8. How many electoral votes did Jimmy Carter receive?
9. John Anderson didn't get any electoral votes. What percentage of the popular vote did he receive?
10. Jimmy Carter won the electoral votes of Washington, D.C., and only a few states. How many?
11. If you answered the last question correctly and you can do simple arithmetic, you should know how many states Reagan carried. How many?
12. Jimmy Carter carried only two states west of the Mississippi. One was his vice president's home state. Which state is that?
13. What other state west of the Mississippi was carried by Jimmy Carter?
14. Carter carried only one state in the Deep South. Which one?
15. Carter carried only two border states. One is a two-word state. What state is that?
16. What other border state was carried by Jimmy Carter?
17. What is the only state that Carter carried in New England?

18. Although Carter lost the traditionally Democratic states of the industrial Northeast, his greatest humiliation was undoutedly his disasterous showing in...In what part of the country?
19. Carter lost many Jewish votes because of his vacillation in regard to...In regard to what?
20. Ronald Reagan is the oldest elected president. True or False?

Ronald Reagan was elected president on November 4, 1980. Reagan is shown in his hotel suite on November 4th, displaying a newspaper headline that pre-maturely declared his victory.

THE 1980 ELECTION QUIZ II

(Score five points for each correct answer.)

1. What phenomenon that was only 5 percent when Carter took office and went up at one point during his administration to 18 percent probably cost him the election more than any other single issue?

2. All during the campaign, the Reagan forces had feared that Carter would pull a last-minute "October surprise." When the surprise came in a somewhat muted form, it probably hurt Carter more than it helped him. What was this so-called surprise?

3. Do most of the political pundits think that Anderson's independent campaign had much influence on the election's outcome?

4. What bloc of voters that was responsible for the unreliability of the pre-election polls turned the tide for Ronald Reagan?

5. American women voted for Reagan in far greater numbers than had been anticipated, confounding the conventional wisdom that they would be susceptible to Carter's charge that Reagan might lead the country into...Into what?

6. Reagan got 54 percent of the male vote. What percentage of the female vote did he receive?

7. Reagan carried many Republican hopefuls to victory, enabling the GOP to gain in the House of Representatives and to actually win control of the Senate for the first time in...In how many years?

8. How many seats did the GOP gain in the Senate?

9. How many seats did the GOP gain in the House?

10. How many governorships did it gain?

11. What took place on Tuesday night, October 28, a week before the election, that apparently swung many undecided voters over to Reagan?

12. On election eve, Ronald Reagan went on national television and asked the American voters a question which they answered the next day by turning Jimmy Carter out of office. What question had Reagan asked?

13. At what hour, Eastern Standard Time, did Carter appear before his unhappy followers and concede defeat?

14. Carter made his concession speech an hour and a quarter before the polls closed in what part of the country?
15. Jimmy Carter was the first Democratic president to be voted out of office since Grover Cleveland. What year was that?
16. While president-elect Reagan received the expected congratulatory phone call from Jimmy Carter, Mr. Reagan also received a surprising phone call from a celebrated Democratic senator who offered his cooperation. Who?
17. At what Los Angeles hotel did Mr. Reagan make his victory speech to wildly enthusiastic supporters?
18. President-elect Reagan's supporters presented him with a cake shaped like...Like what?
19. The cake was festooned with American flags. What did the flags mark?
20. The day after the election, a certain New York market went up dramatically, reflecting considerable faith in the president-elect. What market?

A 1980 Democratic campaign poster.

THE RONALD REAGAN ELECTORAL VOTE QUIZ

Listed on the left below from 1 to 18 are all the 44 states that Ronald Reagan carried in the electoral college. Listed on the right are the number of electoral votes belonging to those states. Match the numbers on the right to the states on the left. Also answer the two questions on Jimmy Carter. (Score five points for each correct answer.)

1.	New York	A.	3
2.	Pennsylvania	B.	4
3.	California	C.	6
4.	Florida, New Jersey	D.	7
5.	Texas, Illinois	E.	8
6.	Ohio	F.	9
7.	Michigan	G.	10
8.	Kanasas, Colorado, Mississippi	H.	11
9.	Wisconsin	I.	12
10.	Tennessee, Louisiana	J.	13
11.	Connecticut, Oklahoma, Iowa, South Carolina	K.	14
12.	Alaska, Vermont, Delaware, North Dakota, Wyoming, Nevada	L.	17
13.	South Dakota, Maine, New Hampshire, Utah, Idaho, New Mexico, Montana	M.	21
14.	Virginia, Missouri	N.	25
15.	Washington, Kentucky, Alabama	O.	26
16.	North Carolina, Indiana	P.	27
17.	Oregon, Arkansas, Arizona	Q.	41
18.	Massachusetts	R.	45

19. Jimmy Carter carried six states in all. What was the only state he carried in New England?
20. In addition to six states, Jimmy Carter carried Washington, D.C. How many electoral votes does it have?

THE "WHO VOTED FOR RONALD REAGAN?" QUIZ

On the left below, American voters are subsumed according to race, religion, occupation, family income, residence and region. The percentage of voters in each group who cast a ballot for Ronald Reagan are listed on the right. Match the percentages on the right to the voters on the left.

(Score five points for each correct answer.)

1.	Whites	A.	36 percent
2.	Blacks	B.	55 percent
3.	Hispanics	C.	14 percent
4.	Catholics	D.	62 percent
5.	Protestants	E.	39 percent
6.	Jews	F.	51 percent
7.	Blue-collar	G.	43 percent
8.	Clerical, white-collar	H.	46 percent
9.	Professional, management	I.	49 percent
10.	Other, including unemployed	J.	56 percent
11.	Low income	K.	49 percent
12.	Middle income	L.	52 percent
13.	High income	M.	38 percent
14.	Suburbanites	N.	48 percent
15.	Small-city dwellers	O.	55 percent
16.	Big-city dwellers	P.	36 percent
17.	Northeast	Q.	56 percent
18.	Midwest	R.	61 percent
19.	South and border states	S.	53 percent
20.	West	T.	54 percent

THE SENATE RACE QUIZ I

(Score five points for each correct answer. And please note: 1 seat in the 100 seats of the Senate is vacant.)

1. When the new Congress convened on January 5, 1981, Republicans were in control of the Senate for the first time since 1954. Is this the 95th, 96th, 97th or 98th Congress?
2. How many seats do the Republicans have?
3. How many seats do the Democrats have?
4. There were 34 Senate seats at stake on November 5, 1980. The Republicans captured 22, the Democrats 12. The Republicans took 12 seats away from the Democrats. How many seats did the Democrats take from the Republicans?

Sixteen of the 34 Senate seats that were in contention on November 5, 1981, are listed below on the left in alphabetical order. The politicians, identified by party, are listed on the right. Match the winners on the right with the states on the left.

5. Alabama   Rep. Jeremiah Denton vs.
                   Dem. James Folsom, Jr.
6. Alaska   Rep. Frank H. Murkowki vs.
                   Dem. Clark Gruening
7. Arizona ·   Rep. Barry Goldwater vs.
                   Dem. W. R. Schulz
8. Arkansas   Rep. William Clark vs.
                   Dem. Dale Bumpers
9. California   Rep. Paul Gann vs.
                   Dem. Alan Cranston
10. Colorado   Rep. Mary Estill Buchanan vs.
                   Dem. Gary Hart
11. Conneticut   Rep. James Buckley vs.
                   Dem. Christopher J. Dodd
12. Florida   Rep. Paula Hawkins vs.
                   Dem. Bill Gunter
13. Georgia   Rep. Mack Mattingly vs.
                   Dem .Herman Talmadge
14. Hawaii   Rep. Cooper Brown vs.
                   Dem. Daniel Inouye
15. Idaho   Rep. Steven D. Symms vs.
                   Dem. Frank Church

THE SENATE RACE QUIZ II

The Senate-seat states not listed in the first quiz are listed below on the left. The politicians, identified by party, are listed on the right. Again, match the winners on the right with the states on the left. Then answer the two bonus questions. (Score five points for each correct answer.)

1. Louisiana   Russell Long, only contestant, won.
Republican or Democrat?

2. Maryland   Rep. Charles Mathias vs.
Dem. E. T. Conroy

3. Missouri   Rep. Gene McNary vs.
Dem. Thomas Eagleton

4. Nevada   Rep. Paul Laxalt vs.
Dem. Mary Cojack

5. New Hampshire   Rep. Warren Rudman vs.
Dem. John Durkin

6. New York   Rep. Alfonse M. D'Amato vs.
Dem. Liz Holtzman

7. North Carolina   Rep. John P. East vs.
Dem. Robert Morgan

8. North Dakota   Rep. Mark Andrews vs.
Dem. Kent Johanneson

9. Ohio   Rep. James Betts vs.
Dem. John Glenn

10. Oklahoma   Rep. Don Nickles vs.
Dem. Andrew Coats

11. Oregon   Rep. Bob Packwood vs.
Dem. Ted Kulongoski

12. Pennsylvania   Rep. Arlen Spector vs.
Dem. Pete Flaherty

13. South Carolina   Rep. Marshall Mays vs.
Dem. Ernest "Fritz" Hollings

14. South Dakota   Rep. James Abdnor vs.
Dem. George McGovern

15. Utah   Rep. Jake Garn vs.
Dem. Dan Berman

16. Vermont   Rep. Stewart Ledbetter vs.
Dem. Patrick J. Leahy

17. Washington   Rep. Slade Gorton vs.
Dem. Warren Magnuson

THE BREAKUP OF THE DEMOCRATIC COALITION QUIZ

(Score five points for each corect answer.)

In order to understand the breakup of the Democratic coalition, it is necessary to understand how its components coalesced in the first place.

Abraham Lincoln was the first Republican president. After his assassination at the end of the Civil War, the radical Republicans imposed a harsh reconstruction on the defeated South, leaving a legacy of bitterness toward the Republican party. The vast majority of white Southerners voted Democratic until well after World War II. The majority of black Americans, on the other hand, were loyal to the party of Lincoln until the presidency of F.D.R. and the rise of the New Deal. It was Roosevelt who created a Democratic coalition out of the most disparate elements in American society: blacks, conservatives, white Southerners, Jews, Catholics, organized labor and liberal intellectuals. The GOP thus became a party primarily composed of business-oriented, northern and midwestern white Protestants, who hardly formed a large enough constituency to win national elections. When Hispanics were added to the American mosaic after World War II they also joined the Democratic party. Indeed, to this day, people who call themselves Democrats outnumber people who call themselves Republicans two-to-one. But what people call themselves and the way they vote are not necessarily the same, as witness the outcome of the 1980 election. The old Democratic coalition had come apart. Why? Well, it was a seemingly impossible coalition to begin with, and the wonder is that it lasted so long. Of course, a pronouncement of its demise may well be premature. About all we can say for certain is that the Democratic party is in trouble.

1. The first sign of Democratic trouble in the post-war years was the election of Dwight D. Eisenhower, whose popularity with the American people cut across party lines. What were the years of Eisenhower's presidency, from the time he took office until the time he left?

2. In the 1960s there was the war in Vietnam, the rise of a counter-culture and the emergence of a generation gap. While many mainstream Democrats remained liberal on economic issues, they were increasingly outraged by war protestors, by the spread of pornography, by the rising crime rate, by hippies, yippies, bra-burners, public fornicators, et al. What was the name of the issue which separated the mainstream Democrats from the advocates of a more permissive life style?

3. True or False? The advocates of women's rights, affirmative action, abortion and environmental causes tended to be drawn from the Democratic party's more affluent and college-educated members, from whom the more socially conservative white working class was increasingly alienated.

4. Actually, the white working class now saw itself as essentially middle-class and felt that traditional American values were being threatened, especially in regard to something that had been called the fundamental societal unit. What is that?

5. What region of the U.S. was beginning to embrace the Republican party in the 1960s?

6. Beginning in the 1960s there was a demographic shift from the old industrial states of the Northeast to the Sunbelt (encompassing the South, the Southwest and California). "Demographic" is a fancy word for what?

7. There was considerable class polarization in the 1960s. The counter-culture young, who tended to be drawn from affluent and relatively liberal upper-middle-class families, derided the old- fashioned patriotism of hard-hat construction workers and taunted lower-middle-class policemen. In what year, in what city, was a Democratic convention thrown into chaos by a so-called police riot, in which yippies and hippies battled with cops on the city's streets?

8. What old-style Democrat was mayor of that city?

9. The so-called police riots and the turmoil within the convention itself, all of which was seen on national television, helped to defeat the Democrats that year. True or False?

10. Who was the Democratic presidential candidate that year?

11. Who was his running mate?
12. The Democrat's campaign of 1972 was marked by incredible bungling from the very beginning. The nomination of George McGovern, who alienated old-style Democrats on the social issue, assured the party's defeat. McGovern chose as his running mate a man who was soon forced to resign. What was his name?
13. He was a U.S. senator from what state?
14. Who, finally, was McGovern's running mate?
15. Nixon, of course, won reelection that year. Who was his running mate?
16. In 1972 there appeared a book entitled The Emerging Republican Majority. Who wrote it?
17. The Republican party received a severe but temporary set-back from a scandal during Nixon's second administration. What was the name of the scandal?
18. Before the 1980 election, it was found that Republican were in greater agreement with the goals of their party than were Democrats on the goals of their party. What issue more than any other hurt the Democrats that year?
19. The two most controversial issues within the Republican party itself were Reagan's proposed tax cut and something regarding the fair sex. What was that?
20. What former Kennedy speechwriter and New Frontiersman said, "The issues of the 1930s are not the issues of the 1980s and the Democrats have confused values with solutions"?

Ronald Reagan meets Representatives Delbert Latta (left), R.-Ohio, and Phil Gramm, D.-Texas, at the White House on May 7, 1981. Gramm and Latta formulated a bipartisan budget bill that reflected Reagan's conservative philosophy.
190 Republican members of the House as well as 63 Democrats voted in favor to win passage of the administration-backed plan.

THE REAGAN-STYLE QUIZ

(Score five points for each correct answer.)

1. What is Nancy's favorite color?
2. Who is her favorite dress designer?
3. What other two designers complete her wardrobe?
4. What type of tobacco product does she particularly detest?
5. What type of stories does she detest?
6. What Beverly Hills epidermal expert has helped keep Nancy's skin flawless for over 20 years?
7. Nancy chats almost daily with a woman named Betsy, the wife of a department-store scion. What's her last name?
8. Her husband founded the Diners Club. What's his name?
9. What celebrated, blue-eyed singer who hasn't been invited to the White House since the Kennedy era is likely to do an encore under the Reagans?
10. What other singer, called "the King of the Roasts," is likely to be invited to the White House?
11. Does Ronald Reagan like to be roasted?
12. What tall, lanky, "aw-shucks" actor and his wife are likely to be invited to the White House?
13. What actress now married to a Virginia senator is an old Hollywood friend of the Reagans?
14. The Reagans closest friends are California entrepreneurs and their wives. Among them are Jack and Bonita Wrather. What was her screen name?
15. Nancy adores fresh flowers . True or False?
16. How does she like her vegetables cooked?
17. Ronald Reagan has two favorite dishes. One of them is an unusual type of lasagne. What type of lasagne?
18. What is Ronald Reagan's other favorite dish?
19. To what type of baked dessert or sweet-treat are both Nancy and Ronald Reagan particularly partial?
20. Not long ago the affable Ronald Reagan spotted Don Rickles and requested something that Rickles uncharacteristically refused to do. What two words did Ronald Reagan say to Don Rickles?

NANCY, OUR NEW FIRST LADY QUIZ I

(Score five points for each correct answer.)

1. What was the prophetic two-word title of Nancy's 1939 high-school senior-class play in which she had the leading role?
2. What is the title of Nancy's autobiography?
3. In what year was Nancy born?
4. What name was she given at birth?
5. What was her father's occupation?
6. What was Nancy's nickname from the beginning?
7. What was Nancy's mother's occupation?
8. What was Nancy's mother's professional name?
9. What did Nancy's father do not long after her birth?
10. At what age was Nancy sent to live with relatives?
11. When Nancy was seven, her mother remarried. Nancy went to live with her mother and stepfather. What was his name?
12. What was his profession?
13. Where did he practice his profession?
14. How old was Nancy when he legally adopted her?
15. At what age was Nancy a debutante?
16. What was the name of the Chicago club in which Nancy made her debut?
17. What high school did Nancy attend?
18. What was Nancy's childhood ambition?
19. What college did Nancy attend?

With their dog "James" for company, President-elect Ronald Reagan and his wife, Nancy, share some time together in northern Virginia after his sweeping election victory.

NANCY, OUR NEW FIRST LADY QUIZ II

(Score five points for each correct answer.)

1. One of Nancy's pet projects as First Lady is likely to involve a form of rehabilitation. What type of rehabilitation?
2. Another one of Nancy's pet projects is an ongoing program called Foster Grandparents that entails matching disadvantaged youngsters with senior citizens. What type of disadvantaged youngsters?
3. What is Nancy's stand in regard to abortion, pre-marital sex and the ERA?
4. What type of beverage that the Carters removed from the White House will Nancy serve to diplomats and other honored guests?
5. What type of wines will Nancy serve in the White House?
6. Nancy likes white wine. What does her husband prefer?
7. Although Nancy and Ronald Reagan drink sparingly, there is a particular type of liquor that they prefer. Is it Scotch, vodka, bourbon, rye or gin?
8. What famous actor, who was a friend of Nancy's family, helped her get a screen test with a major Hollywood studio?
9. What was this major Hollywood studio?
10. In what year did she sign a contract with the studio?

President-elect and Mrs. Ronald Reagan are brought to the stage by their good friend, Frank Sinatra, following the inaugural gala honoring the Reagans at the Washington, D.C. Capital Center.

THE REAGAN FAMILY QUIZ I

(Score five points for each correct answer.)

1. Is Ronald Reagan younger or older than his brother Neil?
2. In what state does Neil live?
3. What was his occupation before he retired?
4. How many grown children does Ronald Reagan have?
5. Ronald Reagan and Jane Wyman had two children. One was adopted. What's his name?
6. How many times has he been married?
7. This adopted son owns a business in California. What's the name of this business?
8. Ronald Reagan also has a daughter from his earlier marriage to Jane Wyman. What is this daughter's name?
9. How many times has she been married and divorced?
10. Is she married now?

First Lady Nancy Reagan peddles away as son, Ron, hams it up during a moment of leisure around the White House South Lawn.

THE REAGAN FAMILY QUIZ II

(Score five points for each correct answer.)

1. What is the name of Nancy and Ronald Reagan's daughter from their own marriage?
2. She is an actress. What is her professional name?
3. What did she do with a member of the Eagles rock group that upset her rather strait-laced mother?
4. What's his name?
5. In what city and state does the Reagan's younger daughter live?
6. What do all four Reagan children have in common vis-a-vis their college careers?
7. Ronald Reagan's adopted son and his wife have given Ronald Reagan his only grandchild. What is the grandchild's name?
8. What is the name of Ronald Reagan's daughter-in-law?
9. Nancy and Ronald Reagan have two homes in California. One is a ranch. What town is it near?
10. What does Ronald Reagan like to do at his ranch that is a good form of exercise and one of his favorite pastimes?
11. Where is the Reagans' other home in California?
12. Nancy Reagan has called herself "a frustrated interior decorator". What type of furniture and paintings does she particularly like?
13. Ronald Reagan drinks very moderately because of his late father. Why?
14. Which of the Reagan children was nicknamed "the Skipper"?
15. To which of his four children did Ronald Reagan write "There is no greater happiness for a man than approaching a door at the end of a day knowing someone on the other side of that door is waiting for the sound of his footsteps"?
16. What was the occasion?
17. In response to an inquiry on "the nicest thing a girl ever did for me," Ronald wrote, "The nicest thing a girl ever did for me was when a girl named Nancy married me and brought a warmth and joy to my life that has grown with each passing year". That was in

1971 when he was governor of California. Who made the inquiry?

18. Although Ronald Reagan is very much in the public eye, he loves to retreat to his ranch because he very much values his...His what?

19. How many acres is the ranch?

20. Who is the person closest to Ronald Reagan?

First Lady Nancy Reagan gives hug and kiss to son, Ron, as the President looks on following their son's performance with the Joffrey II dance company's Washington debut.

Nancy Reagan and Lena Horne get together backstage at the Nederlander Theater in New York City after Miss Horne's performance in "The Lady and Her Music." Looking on are Mrs. Reagan's son Ron and his wife Doria.

RONALD PRESCOTT REAGAN'S MARRIAGE QUIZ

(Score five points for each correct answer.)

On Monday morning, November 25, 1980, less than two weeks after his father was elected president of the United States, Ronald Prescott Reagan married his live-in girlfriend.

1. What was her full maiden name?
2. How long had they been living together before they got married?
3. In what city were they married?
4. What does Ronald Prescott Reagan's wife do for a living?
5. Did they get married in a religious or civil ceremony?
6. Ronald Prescott Reagan was 22 when he got married. How old was his bride?
7. Only two people witnessed the ceremony. One was a friend of the groom. The other was a government agent. What kind of agent?
8. What type of ring was the bride wearing?
9. Was the groom wearing a ring?
10. Was there a honeymoon?
11. The couple took their marriage vows in casual clothes. Which one wore a red sweatshirt, blue jeans and tennis shoes?
12. Which one wore red cowboy boots, a black sweater and black slacks?
13. According to a friend, the marriage was an "elopement". True or False?
14. The couple's neighbors gave them a small party. What type of alchohol was served?
15. At what Los Angeles school were the couple reputed to have met?

THE BROOKE ASTOR PARTY QUIZ I

(Score five points for each correct answer.)

On Tuesday, December 9, 1980, Mrs. Brooke Astor, the Republican philanthropist and social doyenne, held a private dinner party for President-elect Reagan and his wife, Nancy.

1. The party was held in Mrs. Astor's apartment on Manhattan's East Side. On what famous avenue is Mrs. Astor's apartment?
2. Sixty guests were invited, all of whom Mrs. Astor knew personally. As the president of an important foundation, she gets to meet a lot of people. Of what foundation is she president?
3. What brilliant political columnist, who served as Mr. Reagan's unofficial social director in Washington, suggested the party to Mrs. Astor?
4. Was the columnist invited?
5. Did Mrs. Astor consult with Reagan's staff regarding the guest list?

Naturally, many distinguished people were invited to break bread with the Reagans. Some of those people are listed below on the left. Their occupations or professional positions are listed on the right. It's up to you to match them correctly.

6.	Jewel McCabe	A. President of the National Urban League
7.	Felix G. Rohatyn	B. Fashion Designer
8.	Vernon E. Jordan	C. Financier
9.	Arthur Barnes	D. President of 100 Black Men
10.	Oscar de la Renta	E. President of 100 Black Women

THE BROOKE ASTOR PARTY QUIZ II

(Score five points for each correct answer.)

1. Was the New York City mayor, Ed Koch, invited to the party?
2. Was Henry Kissinger invited?
3. Was New York Governor Hugh Carey invited?
4. Was Republican Senator Jake Javits invited?
5. What widow of a former U.S. vice president was invited?
6. The host of NBC's "Today" show was invited. What's his name?
7. What distinguished NBC Evening News anchorman was invited?
8. Was Mike Wallace of CBS invited?
9. How many courses were served at the meal?
10. Sir Fitzroy MacLean was invited. According to Mrs. Astor, Sir Fitzroy is "a great authority on..." On whom?
11. Mrs. Astor, incidentally, has a home in a county just north of New York City. What county is that?
12. Was Daniel Patrick Moynihan invited to Mrs. Astor's party?
13. The same night as Mrs. Astor's dinner party, an annual dance was given at the St. Regis-Sheraton Hotel by Harry H. Platt, the president of a company famous for an art nouveau lamp. What company?
14. Did some of Mrs. Astor's guests go on to the St. Regis?
15. Had Mrs. Astor planned her dinner party for some time or was it rather hastily arranged?
16. Mrs. Astor said that the one thing her otherwise diverse guests had in common was "concern" for a certain municipality. What municipality?

THE QUINTESSENTIAL REAGAN QUIZ

1. How tall is Ronald Reagan?
2. Within five pounds, how much does he weigh?
3. What color are his eyes?
4. Does he or does he not dye his hair?
5. What color is his hair?
6. What color shirt does he always wear with a coat and tie?
7. What type of ties does he usually wear?
8. What does he usually have showing in his breast pocket?
9. What type of garb does he relax in at his ranch?
10. President Reagan is very attached to a big, black animal named Little Man. What type of animal is he and what is his relationship to Ronald Reagan?
11. Does President Reagan have a good sense of humor?
12. What organ of his body has he referred to as a "hamloaf"?
13. Ronald Reagan is a very soft-hearted man. It hurts him to be thought of as a stingy conservative because he is, as he says, "a pushover for a..." For a what?
14. Ronald Reagan usually wears contact lenses. When does he wear regular eye glasses?
15. Although Ronald Reagan is in excellent health, he takes allergy shots. From what type of allergy does he suffer?
16. What type of surgery did he have in 1967?
17. Is President Reagan hard of hearing?
18. What New York congressman and former Buffalo Bills quarterback predicted that President Reagan would be the GOP's Franklin D. Roosevelt?
19. Does President Reagan prefer to tell political or show-biz anecdotes?
20. Ronald Reagan is a millionaire. In addition to the money he made in show business and on the lecture circuit, he came into a small fortune on a business deal. Did it involve the sale of oil, art works, cattle, stocks and bonds or land?

Presidential campaigner Ronald Reagan with staff member.

The President and his favorite food.

PRESIDENT REAGAN'S CABINET QUIZ

(Score five points for each correct answer.)

1. Who is President Reagan's secretary of state?
2. Under whose administration had he served as chief of staff?
3. What is the full name of President Reagan's secretary of defense?
4. The secretary of defense is a lawyer and a patron of the arts. What type of reviews did he used to write for California newspapers?
5. Incidentally, what was the former title of the Defense Department?
6. Who is President Reagan's attorney general?
7. Who is President Reagan's secretary of the treasury?
8. Who is President Reagan's secretary of HUD?
9. HUD is an acronym for what?
10. Who is President Reagan's secretary of health and human services?
11. Who is President Reagan's secretary of commerce?
12. Who is President Reagan's secretary of labor?
13. Who is President Reagan's secretary of transportation?
14. Who is President Reagan's secretary of agriculture?
15. Who is President Reagan's secretary of the interior?
16. Who is President Reagan's energy secretary?
17. Who is President Reagan's secretary of education?
18. Who now heads the CIA?
19. What do the initials CIA represent?
20. Who is Ronald Reagan's budget director?

President Reagan's first cabinet meeting in the White House was held on January 21, 1981. Shown are President Reagan and Secretaries Schweiker, Watt, Haig, and Weinberger.

Cabinet members Watt, Haig, Carlucci and Wright applaud President Reagan during April 28, 1981 meeting.

THE NATION'S CAPITAL QUIZ I

(Score five points for each correct answer.)

1. What does the D.C. in Washington, D.C., stand for?
2. Washington, D.C., is located between what two states?
3. On what river is the nation's capital?
4. Are there more or less than a million people within the city itself?
5. One of the nation's most influential newspapers is published in Washington, D.C. What paper?
6. The District of Columbia was established by Congress in 1790 and 1791. Who selected the site for the "Federal City"?
7. Construction began on the White House in 1792. What other-almost equally famous U.S. building began to go up a year later?
8. Until 1800, the U.S. capital was in another city. What city?
9. Who was the first president inaugurated in Washington, D.C.?
10. In what year did British troops capture the city and burn the Capitol?
11. What is the address of the White House?
12. What famous cemetery is on the Virginia side of the Potomic?
13. What are the three main branches of the federal government?
14. What famous Washington, D.C., building has a dome?
15. What branch of the federal government convenes on Capitol Hill?
16. Of what two legislative bodies is Congress composed?
17. What is the official name of the congressional library?
18. Where are the Declaration of Independence, the Constitution and the Bill of Rights housed?
19. What fashionable residential area in Washington, D.C., was designated as a national monument in 1967?
20. What is the name of the Washington, D.C., professional football team?

THE NATION'S CAPITAL QUIZ II

(Score five points for each correct answer.)

1. Washington, D.C., does not have a subway system. True or False?
2. To what two presidents are there memorial buildings in Washington?
3. For whom did President Lyndon B. Johnson once suggest-most inappropriately that a memorial be built?
4. To what president is there a monument in the nation's capital?
5. In what year were Washingtonians first allowed to vote in presidential elections?
6. What is the name of Washington's famous Shakespearean library?
7. What is the name of its celebrated art gallery?
8. What is the name of the famous U.S. Army hospital in Washington?
9. What is the name of George Washington's home, preserved on the Virginia side of the Potomic?
10. To what Republican senator from Ohio is there a memorial in Washington?
11. What famous federal building is shaped like a five-pointed star?
12. What celebrated Washington institution houses scores of scientific artifacts?
13. What bridge connects Washington with Arlington National Cemetery?
14. What celebrated and beautiful trees bloom every spring in Washington's West Potomic Park?
15. What are Washington's two famous cathedrals?
16. Which is known as the National or Washington Cathedral?
17. What D.C. university was named after a U.S. president?
18. To what is the Brookings Institute devoted?
19. Washington, D.C., was sacked by the British in the War of 1812. In what other war was it threatened by an invasion force?
20. Only one foreigner ever received an hononary citizenship from the U.S. Congress, a man who loved this country second only to his own and at whose funeral "The Battle Hymn of the Republic" was played, as he had requested. Who was he?

THE FIRST LADIES QUIZ I

Listed below on the left are the first 20 presidents of the United States. The maiden names of their First Ladies-or lack thereof-are listed on the right. Match them.

(Score five points for each correct answer.)

1.	George Washington	A.	Julia Boggs Dent. Lived with hubby in a tent (during the Civil War).
2.	John Adams	B.	Anna Tuthill. Although alive when her husband took office, she stayed in Ohio.
3.	Thomas Jefferson	C.	Louisa Catherine Johnson
4.	James Madison	D.	Martha Wayles
5.	James Monroe	E.	Martha Danbridge
6.	John Quincy Adams	F.	Rachel Donelson. Died before husband took office.
7.	Andrew Jackson	G.	Dolley ("Dolly") Paine
8.	Martin Van Buren	H.	Elizabeth Kortright
9.	William Henry Harrison	I.	Only president who never married.
10.	John Tyler	J.	Elizabeth McCardle, wife of only president ever impeached.
11.	James Knox Polk	K.	Mary Ann Todd
12.	Zachary Taylor	L.	Margaret Mackell Smith
13.	Millard Fillmore	M.	President had two First Ladies in White House. Letitia Christian who died and Julia Gardiner, 24 years old.
14.	Franklin Pierce	N.	This president was a widower for 18 years when he entered the Executive Mansion.
15.	James Buchanan	O.	Lucretia Rudolph, Second First Lady whose husband was assassinated.

16.	Abraham Lincoln	P.	Abigail Smith. The only First Lady to mother a future U.S. president.
17.	Andrew Johnson	Q.	Sarah Childress
18.	Ulysses S. Grant	R.	Abigail Powers. Very sickly First Lady. Assigned official duties to daughter.
19.	Rutherford B. Hayes	S.	Jane Means Appleton. Most tragic First Lady. Three sons died in infancy. The fourth son was killed in a train accident. Spent White House years in reclusion.
20.	James A. Garfield	T.	Lucy Ware Webb. "Lemonade" Lucy banished wine from the White House and started annual Easter egg-rolling contest.

First Lady Nancy Reagan strikes an official White House pose.

THE FIRST LADIES QUIZ II

(Score five points for each correct answer.)

1.	Chester Alan Arthur	A.	Two First Ladies in White House. Ellen Louise Axson died. President married Edith Bolling Galt.
2.	Grover Cleveland	B.	Helen Herron nicknamed "Nellie," sponsored the planting of Japanese cherry trees in Washington.
3.	Benjamin Harrison	C.	Florence Kling
4.	William McKinley	D.	Francis Folsom at age 22, the youngest First Lady and the first who married in the White House.
5.	Theodore Roosevelt	E.	Ida Saxton. Was subject to epiletic fits.
6.	William Howard Taft	F.	Caroline (Carrie) Scott. Died in White House on October 25, 1892.
7.	Woodrow Wilson	G.	Edith Kermit Carow. Mother of "Princess Alice," who married Nicholas Longworth.
8.	Warren G. Harding	H.	Lou Henry
9.	Calvin Coolidge	I.	Claudia Alta Taylor
10.	Herbert Hoover	J.	Elizabeth Virginia Wallace
11.	Franklin D. Roosevelt	K.	Anna Eleanor Roosevelt
12.	Harry S. Truman	L.	Grace Goodhue
13.	Dwight D. Eisenhower	M.	Mamie Geneva Doud
14.	John F. Kennedy	N.	Jacqueline Lee Bouvier
15.	Lyndon B. Johnson	O.	President was a widower.

MIDDLE NAMES OF THE U.S. PRESIDENTS QUIZ

Not all American presidents have had middle names. Twenty who have had middle names are listed on the left, minus their middle names. Their middle names are listed on the right. Match them.

(Score five points for each correct answer.)

1.	Ronald Reagan	A.	Clark
2.	William Harrison	B.	Alan
3.	James Polk	C.	Quincy
4.	Gerald Ford	D.	Baines
5.	Richard Nixon	E.	Grover
6.	Chester Arthur	F.	David
7.	Franklin Roosevelt	G.	Knox
8.	Lyndon Johnson	H.	Rudolph
9.	Herbert Hoover	I.	Woodrow
10.	John Kennedy	J.	Wilson
11.	William Taft	K.	Milhous
12.	Dwight Eisenhower	L.	Howard
13.	Thomas Wilson	M.	Delano
14.	Warren Harding	N.	Fitzgerald
15.	John Coolidge	O.	Henry
16.	Ulysses Grant	P.	Birchard
17.	Rutherford Hayes	Q.	Abram
18.	James Garfield	R.	Simpson
19.	Stephen Cleveland	S.	Gamaliel
20.	John Adams (the sixth president)	T.	Calvin

THE SUPREME COURT QUIZ

(Score five points for each correct answer.)

1. Only one man was ever both president of the United States and a Supreme Court justice. Who was he?
2. No woman has ever sat on the highest court in the land and only one black man has. Who?
3. True or False? A person needs a law degree to sit on the Supreme Court.
4. Since 1869 the Supreme Court has been composed of nine members. Is that number fixed by law?
5. What 20th-century U.S. president was accused of trying to "pack" the Court?

Since the inception of the Supreme Court, there have been 14 chief justices and one man appointed to that position who was rejected. Their dates of service and the presidents who appointed them are listed on the left. The chief justices themselves are listed on the right. Match them.

6. 1789-1795: Washington   A. Frederick Moore Vinson

7. Appointed by Washing-   B. Earl Warren
    ton, but rejected

8. 1796-1800: Washington   C. Melville Weston Fuller

9. 1801-1835: John Adams   D. Oliver Ellsworth

10. 1836-1864: Jackson   E. John Rutledge

11. 1864-1873: Lincoln   F. Harlan Fiske Stone

12. 1874-1888: Grant   G. John Marshall

13. 1888-1910: Cleveland   H. Warren Earl Burger

14. 1910-1921: Taft   I. Roger Brooke Taney

15. 1921-1930: Harding   J. Morrison Remick Waite

16. 1930-1941: Hoover   K. Charles Evans Hughes

17. 1941-1946: Roosevelt   L. Edward Douglass White

18. 1946-1953: Truman   M. William Howard Taft

19. 1953-1969: Eisenhower   N. John Jay

20. 1969-Present: Nixon   O. Salmon Portland Chase

THE PRESIDENTIAL QUIZ I

Ronald Reagan is the 40th president of the United States. Listed below on the left are the dates the first 20 presidents took office (rather than when they were elected) and the dates when they actually left office. On the right are the president's names. Match the names on the right to the dates on the left.

(Score five points for each correct answer.)

1.	1789-1797	A.	James Buchanan
2.	1797-1801	B.	Ulysses S. Grant
3.	1801-1809	C.	Martin Van Buren
4.	1809-1817	D.	James Knox Polk
5.	1817-1825	E.	William Henry Harrison
6.	1825-1829	F.	Zachary Taylor
7.	1829-1837	G.	Millard Fillmore
8.	1837-1841	H.	John Tyler
9.	1841	I.	James Monroe
10.	1841-1845	J.	George Washington
11.	1845-1849	K.	Andrew Johnson
12.	1849-1850	L.	Thomas Jefferson
13.	1850-1853	M.	James Madison
14.	1853-1857	N.	Andrew Jackson
15.	1857-1861	O.	Chester A. Arthur
16.	1861-1865	P.	Rutherford B. Hayes
17.	1865-1869	Q.	Abraham Lincoln
18.	1869-1877	R.	John Adams
19.	1877-1881	S.	John Quincy Adams
20.	1881-1885	T.	Franklin Pierce

PRESIDENTIAL QUIZ II

Listed below on the left are the years in office of the last 20 presidents of the United States. Listed on the right are the president's names. Don't be confused by the fact that Grover Cleveland is listed twice. As he served two unconnected terms, he is considered by historians to have conducted, in effect, two different presidencies. Again, match the names on the right to the years on the left.

(Score five points for each correct answer.)

1.	1885	A.	Richard M. Nixon
2.	1885-1889	B.	Harry S. Truman
3.	1889-1893	C.	Woodrow Wilson
4.	1893-1897	D.	Franklin D. Roosevelt
5.	1897-1901	E.	Gerald Ford
6.	1901-1909	F.	Theodore Roosevelt
7.	1909-1913	G.	Warren G. Harding
8.	1913-1921	H.	Herbert Hoover
9.	1921-1923	I.	Grover Cleveland
10.	1923-1929	J.	Grover Cleveland
11.	1929-1933	K.	James Garfield
12.	1933-1945	L.	Dwight D. Eisenhower
13.	1945-1953	M.	Lyndon Baines Johnson
14.	1953-1961	N.	Ronald Reagan
15.	1961-1963	O.	Jimmy Carter
16.	1963-1969	P.	William Howard Taft
17.	1969-1974	Q.	Benjamin Harrison
18.	1974-1977	R.	William McKinley
19.	1977-1981	S.	John F. Kennedy
20.	1981-?	T.	Calvin Coolidge

THE VICE PRESIDENTIAL QUIZ I

George Bush is the 42nd vice president of the United States. His immediate predecessor in that office was Walter Mondale. Thus far, 12 vice presidents have gone on to assume the highest office in the land. Listed on the left below are the first 20 vice presidents of the U.S. The presidents under whom they served are listed on the right. Match the names on the right to those on the left.

(Score five points for each correct answer.)

1.	John Adams *C*	A.	Abraham Lincoln had two vice presidents
2.	Thomas Jefferson *P*	B.	U. S. Grant had two vice presidents
3.	Aaron Burr *G*	C.	George Washington
4.	George Clinton *H*	D.	Abraham Lincoln
5.	Elbridge Gerry *I*	E.	James Buchanan
6.	Daniel D. Tompkins *Q*	F.	Franklin Pierce
7.	John Caldwell Calhoun *K*	G.	Thomas Jefferson
8.	Martin Van Buren *J*	H.	Thomas Jefferson James Madison
9.	Richard Mentor Johnson *L*	I.	James Madison
10.	John Tyler *M*	J.	Andrew Jackson
11.	George Mifflin Dallas *O*	K.	J. Q. Adams Andrew Jackson
12.	Millard Fillmore *N*	L.	Martin Van Buren
13.	William Rufus Devane King *F*	M.	William Henry Harrison
14.	John C. Breckinridge *E*	N.	Zachary Taylor
15.	Hannibal Hamlin *A*	O.	James K. Polk
16.	Andrew Johnson *A*	P.	John Adams
17.	Schuyler Colfax *B*	Q.	James Monroe

18. Henry Wilson *B*   R. James Garfield
19. William Almon Wheeler S. John Adams
20. Chester Alan Arthur *R* T. George Washington

President Ronald Reagan is applauded by Vice-President George Bush and House Speaker Thomas P. (Tip) O'Neill as he delivers his economic message to Congress on February 18, 1981.

THE VICE PRESIDENTIAL QUIZ II

Listed below on the left are the vice presidents from 1885 to 1977. The presidents under whom they served are listed on the right. Match them.

(Score five points for each correct answer.)

1. Thomas Andrews Hendricks S
2. Levi Parsons Morton E
3. Adlai Ewing Stevenson T
4. Garret Augustus Hobart K
5. Theodore Roosevelt L
6. Charles Warren Fairbanks A
7. James Stoolcraft Sherman H
8. Thomas Riley Marshall R
9. Calvin Coolidge Q
10. Charles Gates Dawes P
11. Charles Curtis M
12. John Nance Garner B
13. Henry A. Wallace C
14. Harry S. Truman D
15. Alben William Barkley U
16. Richard Milhous Nixon J
17. Lyndon Baines Johnson I
18. Hubert H. Humphrey, Jr. G
19. Spiro Theodore Agnew N
20. Nelson D. Rockefeller O

A. Theordore Roosevelt
B. Franklin D. Roosevelt
C. Franklin D. Roosevelt
D. Franklin D. Roosevelt
E. Benjamin Harrison
F. William Howard Taft
G. Lyndon Baines Johnson
H. Gerald Ford
I. John F. Kennedy
J. Dwight D. Eisenhower
K. William McKinley
L. William McKinley
M. Herbert Hoover
N. Richard Nixon
O. Richard Nixon
P. Calvin Coolidge
Q. Warren G. Harding
R. Woodrow Wilson
S. Grover Cleveland
T. Grover Cleveland
U. Harry S. Truman

THE STATES OF THE PRESIDENTS QUIZ I

The 40 presidents of the U.S. have come from 18 states. The first 20 presidents, listed below on the left, came from 9 different states. These states are listed below on the right. Match them to the names on the left.

(Score five points for each correct answer.)

1. George Washington *A*
2. John Adams *B*
3. Thomas Jefferson *A*
4. James Madison *A*
5. James Monroe *A*
6. John Quincy Adams *B*
7. Andrew Jackson *C*
8. Martin Van Buren *D*
9. William Henry Harrison *A*
10. John Tyler *A*
11. James Knox Polk *E*
12. Zachary Taylor *A*
13. Millard Fillmore *D*
14. Franklin Pierce *F*
15. James Buchanan *G*
16. Abraham Lincoln *H*
17. Andrew Johnson *E*
18. Ulysses Simpson Grant *I*
19. Rutherford Birchard Hayes *I*
20. James Abram Garfield *I*

A. Virginia
B. Massachusetts
C. South Carolina
D. New York
E. North Carolina
F. New Hampshire
G. Pennsylvania
H. Kentucky
I. Ohio

THE STATES OF THE PRESIDENTS QUIZ II

The last 20 presidents of the U.S. have come from 13 different states. The states are listed below on the right. Match them to the names on the left.

(Score five points for each correct answer.)

1.	Chester Alan Arthur *A*	A.	Vermont *A*
2.	Stephen Grover Cleveland *B*	B.	New Jersey *I*
3.	Benjamin Harrison *C*	C.	Ohio
4.	Stephen Grover Cleveland *D*	D.	New York
5.	William McKinley *C*	E.	Virginia
6.	Theodore Roosevelt *D*	F.	Iowa
7.	William Howard Taft *C*	G.	Missouri
8.	Thomas Woodrow Wilson *E*	H.	Illinois
9.	Warren Gamaliel Harding *C*	I.	Georgia
10.	John Calvin Coolidge *A*	J.	Nebraska
11.	Herbert Clark Hoover *F*	K.	California
12.	Franklin Delano Roosevelt *D*	L.	Texas
13.	Harry S. Truman *G*	M.	Massachusetts
14.	Dwight David Eisenhower *L*		
15.	John Fitzgerald Kennedy *M*		
16.	Lyndon Baines Johnson *L*		
17.	Richard Milhous Nixon *K*		
18.	Gerald Rudolph Ford *J*		
19.	Jimmy Carter *I*		
20.	Ronald Wilson Reagan *H*		

President Reagan carried 44 states in the electoral college while Jimmy Carter carried 6. Listed below on the left are 20 of the states carried by Reagan. Some of their well-known nicknames are on the right. Match them.

(Score five points for each correct answer.)

1. Alabama I	A. Wolverine State
2. Alaska K	B. Land of Lincoln
3. Arizona J	C. Centennial State
4. Arkansas O	D. Blue Hen State
5. California P	E. Hawkeye State
6. Colorado C	F. Sunshine State
7. Connecticut M	G. Hoosier State
8. Delaware D	H. Spud State
9. Florida F	I. Cotton State
10. Idaho H	J. Grand Canyon State
11. Illinois B	K. The Last Frontier
12. Indiana G	L. Jayhawk State
13. Iowa E	M. Nutmeg State
14. Kansas L	N. Magnolia State
15. Kentucky R	O. Wonder State
16. Louisiana T	P. Golden State
17. Maine S	Q. Bay State
18. Massachusetts Q	R. Blue Grass State
19. Michigan A	S. Pine Tree State
20. Mississippi N	T. Creole State

RONALD REAGAN'S ELECTORAL STATES' NICKNAMES QUIZ II

(Score five points for each correct answer.)

1.	Missouri J	A.	Green Mountain State
2.	Montana I	B.	Tar Heel State
3.	Nebraska G	C.	Volunteer State
4.	Nevada M	D.	Palmetto State
5.	New Hampshire O	E.	Keystone State
6.	New Jersey P	F.	Beaver State
7.	New Mexico S	G.	Cornhuskers State
8.	New York K	H.	Buckeye State
9.	North Carolina B	I.	Treasure State
10.	North Dakota T	J.	Show-Me State
11.	Ohio H	K.	Empire State
12.	Oklahoma N	L.	Lone Star State
13.	Oregon F	M.	Sagebrush State
14.	Pennsylvania E	N.	Sooner State
15.	South Carolina D	O.	Granite State
16.	South Dakota Q	P.	Garden State
17.	Tennessee C	Q.	Coyote State
18.	Texas L	R.	Beehive State
19.	Utah R	S.	Cactus State
20.	Vermont A	T.	Sioux State

95

RONALD REAGAN'S ELECTORAL STATES' CAPITAL QUIZ I

Ronald Reagan carried 44 states in the electoral college while Jimmy Carter carried 6. Listed below on the left are 20 of the states carried by Reagan. Their capitals, many of which he visited, are on the right. Match them.

(Score five points for each correct answer.)

1. Alabama *H*	A. Lansing
2. Alaska *J*	B. Jackson
3. Arizona *L*	C. Topeka
4. Arkansas *N*	D. Boston
5. California *O*	E. Augusta
6. Colorado *P*	F. Baton Rouge
7. Connecticut *T*	G. Frankfurt
8. Delaware *S*	H. Montgomery
9. Florida *R*	I. Des Moines
10. Idaho *Q*	J. Juneau
11. Illinois *M*	K. Indianapolis
12. Indiana *K*	L. Phoenix
13. Iowa *I*	M. Springfield
14. Kansas *C*	N. Little Rock
15. Kentucky *G*	O. Sacramento
16. Louisiana *F*	P. Denver
17. Maine *E*	Q. Boise
18. Massachusetts *D*	R. Tallahassee
19. Michigan *A*	S. Dover
20. Mississippi *B*	T. Hartford

RONALD REAGAN'S ELECTORAL STATES' CAPITALS QUIZ II

(Score five points for each correct answer.)

1. Missouri *F*
2. Montana *G*
3. Nebraska *J*
4. Nevada *K*
5. New Hampshire *L*
6. New Jersey *N*
7. New Mexico *S*
8. New York *M*
9. North Carolina *O*
10. North Dakota *P*
11. Ohio *I*
12. Oklahoma *H*
13. Oregon *E*
14. Pennsylvania *R*
15. South Carolina *T*
16. South Dakota *Q*
17. Tennessee *C*
18. Texas *D*
19. Utah *A*
20. Vermont *B*

A. Salt Lake City
B. Montpelier
C. Nashville
D. Austin
E. Salem
F. Jefferson City
G. Helena
H. Oklahoma City
I. Columbus
J. Lincoln
K. Carson City
L. Concord
M. Albany
N. Trenton
O. Raleigh
P. Bismarck
Q. Pierre
R. Harrisburg
S. Santa Fe
T. Columbia

THE RONALD REAGAN U.S. HISTORY QUIZ I

Ronald Wilson Reagan, the 40th president of the United States, is now an irrevocable part of American history and government which, in its unbroken continuity, is one of the oldest on earth. Listed below on the left are 20 highlights-both good and bad-in American history. Their dates are listed on the right. Match them.

(Score five points for each correct answer.)

1.	Emancipation Proclamation	A.	1865
2.	The American Revolution	B.	1963
3.	The Census declares the frontier closed	C.	1964
4.	The Battle of the Little Big Horn	D.	1964
5.	Assassination of Lincoln	E.	1903
6.	Assassination of John F. Kennedy	F.	1775-
7.	The Louisiana Purchase		1781
8.	The Civil War	G.	1890
9.	The Declaration of Independence	H.	1876
10.	The U.S. Moon Landing	I.	1954
11.	American involvement in World War II	J.	1776
12.	The Great Stock Market Crash	K.	1803
13.	The Wright Brothers invent the airplane	L.	1803
14.	The Gulf of Tonkin Resolution and the American build-up in Vietnam	M.	1787
15.	The coming of the New Deal	N.	1789
16.	American involvement in the Great War	P.	1945
17.	The Atom Bomb	Q.	1933
18.	The drafting of the Constitution	R.	1941-
19.	The Bill of Rights		1945
20.	The Supreme Court decision outlawing segregation in U.S. public schools	S.	1863
		T.	1929

THE RONALD REAGAN U.S. HISTORY QUIZ II

(Score five points for each correct answer.)

1.	End of southern Reconstruction	A.	1620
2.	Columbus discovers America	B.	1626
3.	Andrew Jackson beats the British at the Battle of New Orleans	C.	1804
4.	The completion of the Erie Canal	D.	1825
5.	The election of Andrew Jackson	E.	1859
6.	The official beginning of national prohibition	F.	1857
7.	Mark Twain publishes Huckleberry Finn	G.	1855
8.	The Spanish-American War	H.	1828
9.	The Battle of Wounded Knee and the end of the Indian wars	I.	1773
10.	Walt Whitman publishes Leaves of Grass	J.	1820
11.	The Missouri Compromise	K.	1877
12.	The battle of Lexington and Concord	L.	1925
13.	The Boston Tea Party	M.	1920
14.	The Dred Scott Decision	N.	1775
15.	John Brown attacks Harpers Ferry	O.	1898
16.	The Lewis and Clark Expedition begins	P.	1862
17.	Peter Minuit purchases Manhattan from the Indians	Q.	1884
18.	F. Scott Fitzgerald publishes The Great Gatsby	R.	1890
19.	The Homestead Act	S.	1815
20.	The Pilgrims land at Plymouth Rock	T.	1492

THE FIRST REPUBLICAN PRESIDENT QUIZ

(Score five points for each correct answer.)

It is interesting to note that Ronald Reagan is the 16th Republican president and that Abraham Lincoln, the first Republican to occupy the White House, was the 16th president!

One of our greatest presidents, Lincoln, has captured the imagination of the American people. A strong but gentle man, and perhaps the only American president who ever had the soul of a poet, Lincoln broodingly presided over the Civil War, that tragic conflict in which more Americans lost their lives than in the two world wars combined.

1. Although he was born and grew to manhood in another state, Illinois is called "The Land of Lincoln". Why?
2. It is well known that Lincoln was born in a log cabin. In what state was he born?
3. What was the date of his birth?
4. What was his father's given name?
5. What was his mother's maiden name?
6. To what town in Illinois did he move in 1837?
7. What type of professional occupation did he practice there?
8. Did he have a degree in that profession?
9. What elective office did he hold in Washington, D.C., from 1847 to 1849?
10. What office did he unsuccessfully seek in 1858?
11. With whom did he engage that year in what became a series of great historic debates?
12. Lincoln had married in 1842. What was his wife's maiden name?
13. In what year was Lincoln first elected president of the United States?
14. True or False? Although the South succeeded in response to Lincoln's election and the argument over slavery, the primary reason that Lincoln led the North into war was not to free the slaves but to preserve the Union.
15. What were the years of the Civil War?

16. In what year did Lincoln issue the Emancipation Proclamation?
17. By whom was Lincoln assassinated at the end of the Civil War?
18. In what theatre was Lincoln assassinated?
19. What play was he watching at the time?
20. At Lincoln's death, his secretary of war quietly proclaimed, "Now he belongs to the ages". Who was Lincoln's secretary of war?

Senate Minority Leader Everett Dirksen gives some important pointers to two possible Republican presidential candidates, Governor Ronald Reagan of California and Senator Charles Percy of Illinois in 1967.

AMERICAN POLITICAL PARTIES QUIZ

(Score five points for each correct answer.)

1. What animal is the symbol of the Republican party?
2. What animal is the symbol of the Democratic party?
3. Who was the first Republican president and in what year was he first elected?
4. Who was the first president under the modern Democratic party and in what year was he first elected?
5. When George Washington first became president, there were no American political parties. What party did he represent when he won reelection in 1792?
6. What was Thomas Jefferson's political party?
7. In 1848 Zachary Taylor was the last president elected as the leader of a party with a four-letter name. What party?
8. What was the name of the party that competed with the Republican and Democratic parties in the elections of 1876, 1880 and 1884?
9. To what party did silver-tongued William Jennings Bryan, the three-time presidential loser, belong?
10. Labor leader Euguene V. Debs ran for the presidency five times. What was his political party?
11. Who was the first Roman Catholic presidential candidate, what was his party and in what year did he run for president?
12. What was Strom Thurmond's political party when he ran for president in 1948?
13. Who ran for president as a Progressive in 1948?
14. With what party was Teddy Roosevelt associated when elected president in 1904?
15. Following an argument with the Old Guard Republicans, Teddy Roosevelt bolted from the GOP and ran as the first Progressive party candidate in 1912. Who won the presidency that year and what was his party?
16. In 1912 the Progressive party was nicknamed after a large, strong animal to which the ever ebullient Teddy Roosevelt compared himself. What animal?
17. What was the name of the scandal that the Republican party endured under President Warren G. Harding in 1923?

18. To what party did Norman Thomas belong?
19. In 1968 George C. Wallace made a third-party bid as an American Independent. Who was his running mate?
20. To what political party did President Reagan belong for the greater part of his adult life?

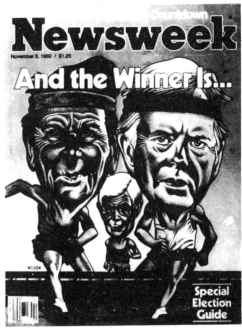

The Presidential candidates shown in *U.S. News & World Report* and *Newsweek.*

Listed on the left below are 20 presidential winners, their running mates and the years in which they were elected. Listed on the right are their major opponents and their running mates. Match the losers on the right to the winners on the left.

(Score five points for each correct answer.)

1. 1804: Thomas Jefferson George Clinton	A.	Adlai Stevenson Estes Kefauver
2. 1812: James Madison Elbridge Gerry	B.	Grover Cleveland Allen G. Thurman
3. 1816: James Monroe Daniel D. Tompkins	C.	Charles C. Daniel Rufus King
4. 1828: Andrew Jackson John C. Calhoun	D.	Rufus King John E. Howard
5. 1836: Martin Van Buren Richard M. Johnson	E.	DeWitt Clinton Jared Ingersoll
6. 1860: Abraham Lincoln Hannibal Hamlin	F.	William H.Harrison Francis Granger
7. 1864: Abraham Lincoln Andrew Johnson	G.	John Quincy Adams Richard Rush
8. 1888: Benjamin Harrison Levi P. Morton	H.	Charles Evan Hughes Charels W. Fairbanks
9. 1900: William McKinley Theodore Roosevelt	I.	Barry Goldwater William E. Miller
10. 1908: William Howard Taft James S. Sherman	J.	Thomas E. Dewey Earl Warren
11. 1916: Woodrow Wilson Thomas R. Marshall	K.	Thomas E. Dewey John W. Bricker
12. 1920: Warren G. Harding Calvin Coolidge	L.	Alfred E. Smith Joseph T. Robinson
13. 1928: Herbert Hoover Charles Curtis	M.	Alfred M. Landon Frank Knox
14. 1936: Franklin D. Roosevelt John Nance Garner	N.	Wendell Wilkie Charles McNary
15. 1940: Franklin D. Roosevelt Henry Wallace	O.	James M. Cox Franklin D. Roosevelt
16. 1944: Franklin D. Roosevelt Harry S. Truman	P.	William Jennings Bryan John W. Kern
17. 1948: Harry S. Truman Alben W. Barkley	Q.	William Jennings Bryan Adlai E. Stevenson

18. 1952: Dwight D. Eisenhower R. George McClellan
            Richard M. Nixon   George Pendleton
19. 1956: Dwight D. Eisenhower S. Stephen A. Douglas
            Richard M. Nixon   Herschel V. Johnson
20. 1964: Lyndon B. Johnson   T. Adlai Stevenson
            Hubert H. Humphrey   John Sparkman

The Presidential Inaugural Committee
requests the honor of your presence
to attend and participate in the Inauguration of
Ronald Wilson Reagan
as President of the United States of America
and
George Herbert Walker Bush
as Vice President of the United States of America
on Tuesday the twentieth of January
one thousand nine hundred and eighty one
in the City of Washington

The "Official" Presidential Inaugural Invitation.

PRESIDENTIAL OCCUPATIONS QUIZ

Listed below on the left are 20 U.S. presidents. Some of their former occupations are listed on the right. Match them.

(Score five points for each correct answer.)

1. George Washington	A.	Newspaper editor and publisher
2. John Adams	B.	Soldier, university president
3. Thomas Jefferson	C.	Lawyer, university president
4. Andrew Jackson	D.	Surveyor, soldier, planter
5. William H. Harrison	E.	Teacher, lawyer
6. Abraham Lincoln	F.	Peanut farmer
7. Andrew Johnson	G.	Planter, lawyer
8. U. S. Grant	H.	Planter, lawyer, soldier
9. James Garfield	I.	Soldier, planter
10. Chester A. Arthur	J.	Film actor
11. Theodore Roosevelt	K.	Tailor
12. Woodrow Wilson	L.	Soldier, farmer, clerk
13. Warren G. Harding	M.	Lawyer
14. Herbert Hoover	N.	Laborer, professor
15. Harry S. Truman	O.	School teacher, lawyer
16. Dwight D. Eisenhower	P.	Historian, rancher
17. John F. Kennedy	Q.	Engineer, relief administrator
18. Lyndon B. Johnson	R.	Habersdaher
19. Jimmy Carter	S.	Author, reporter
20. Ronald Reagan	T.	School teacher

PRESIDENTIAL RELIGION QUIZ

(Score five points for each correct answer.)

1. Ten U.S. presidents have belonged to a Protestant denomination that is the American version of England's Anglican Church. What denomination?
2. Seven U.S. presidents have belonged to a Protestant denomination that was founded by John Calvin. What denomination?
3. Jimmy Carter was a born-again Christian, but what was his denomination?
4. What was Gerald Ford's denomination?
5. To what church did Lyndon Johnson belong?
6. What 20th-century president was a member of the Dutch Reformed Church?
7. What was Franklin D. Roosevelt's denominaton?
8. True or False? Thomas Jefferson was an Episcopalian.
9. True or False? President Reagan had a Catholic father and a Protestant mother.
10. William McKinley belonged to a Protestant denomination that was founded in England by John Wesley. What denomination?

Listed below on the left are the religions of 10 U.S. presidents. The presidents themselves are listed on the right. Match them with their religions.

11. Quaker	A. George Washington
12. Dutch Reformed	B. John Adams
13. Baptist	C. Andrew Jackson
14. Presbyterian	D. Martin Van Buren
15. Unitarian	E. Abraham Lincoln
16. Episcopalian	F. U. S. Grant
17. Roman Catholic	G. Warren G. Harding
18. Congregationalist	H. Calvin Coolidge
19. Methodist	I. Herbert Hoover
20. No formal religious affiliation	J. John F. Kennedy

THE PRESIDENTIAL POTPOURRI QUIZ I

(Score five points for each correct answer.)

1. Who was the only U.S. president who had a Ph.D.?
2. What two presidents were fifth cousins?
3. What president held "fireside chats" with the American people?
4. Who was the first president to be limited to two terms by the 22nd constitutional amendment?
5. What future president wrote a bestselling book entitled Why England Slept?
6. Who was the first Democratic president after the Civil War?
7. Who was the only former U.S. president to become a senator?
8. What two presidents other than Lincoln and Kennedy were assassinated?
9. Who assassinated them?
10. Who (apparently) assassinated John Kennedy?
11. Who killed President Kennedy's apparent assassin?
12. Who killed President Kennedy's brother Bobby?
13. Turning to the lighter side, who was the heaviest president and how much did he weigh?
14. Who was the tallest president and what was his height?
15. Who was the first president who had married a divorcee?
16. Who was the first divorced president?
17. What three U.S. presidents were sons of clergymen?
18. What president has been called "the secular American Christ"?
19. What two presidents won Nobel Peace Prizes?
20. Who was the first U.S. president to wear long trousers?

THE PRESIDENTIAL POTPOURRI QUIZ II

(Score five points for each correct answer.)

1. Who was the youngest president ever inaugurated and how old was he?
2. Who was the second youngest president ever inaugurated and how old was he?
3. Who was the oldest president ever inaugurated and how old was he?
4. Who was the second oldest president ever inaugurated and how old was he?
5. The oldest ex-president lived to the age of 91. Who was he?
6. What 20th-century president lived to the ripe, old age of 90?
7. How old was Harry Truman when he died?
8. How old was Eisenhower when he died?
9. What three presidents other than Lincoln were actually born in a log cabin?
10. What president was never convinced that the earth was round instead of flat?
11. Which two former presidents died on July 4, 1826, 50 years to the day after they signed the Declaration of Independence?
12. What future president drafted the Declaration of Independence?
13. Who was the first president to be photographed while in office?
14. "Tippecanoe and Tyler too!" was the campaign slogan of what president?
15. Who was the only U.S. president to marry the same woman twice?
16. What two presidents suffered from gout?
17. William Henry Harrison served only one month as U.S. president. Of what disease did he die?
18. What father and son were U.S. presidents?
19. What grandfather and grandson were U.S. presidents?
20. Who was the only U.S. president who was not sworn in on a Bible?

COLLEGES OF THE PRESIDENTS QUIZ

Listed below on the left are 20 American presidents. Their colleges are listed on the right. Match them.

(Score five points for each correct answer.)

1. Ronald Reagan *N*   A. Kenyon College
                                  Harvard Law School
2. Jimmy Carter *P*   B. William and Mary
3. Gerald R. Ford *T*   C. Didn't go to college
4. Richard Nixon *Q*   D. Stanford University
5. Lyndon B. Johnson *S*   E. Union College
6. John F. Kennedy *K*   F. Yale, Cincinnati Law School
7. Dwight D. Eisenhower *O*   G. Amherst College
8. Harry S. Truman *C*   H. Ohio Central College
9. Franklin D. Roosevelt *R* I. Princeton, John Hopkins
10. Herbert Hoover *D*   J. Williams College,
                                  Professorship at Hiram
                                  College
11. Calvin Coolidge *K*   K. Harvard
12. Warren G. Harding   L. Hampden-Sidney College
13. Woodrow Wilson   M. Bowdoin College
14. William Howard Taft *N*   N. Eureka College
15. James A. Garfield *J*   O. West Point
16. Chester A. Arthur   P. Annapolis
17. Rutherford B. Hayes *A*   Q. Whittier College, Duke
                                  University Law School
18. Franklin Pierce *M*   R. Harvard, Columbia Law
19. William H. Harrison *H*   S. Southwest Texas State
                                  College
20. Thomas Jefferson *B*   T. University of Michigan,
                                  Yale Law School

PARENTS OF THE PRESIDENTS QUIZ

Listed below on the left are the first names of the fathers and the maiden names of the mothers of 20 presidents. The presidents themselves are listed on the right. Match them.

(Score five points for each correct answer.)

1. Mary Ball and Augustine T   A. Ronald Reagan
2. Dorothy Gardner and Gerald C   B. Jimmy Carter
3. Phoebe Dickerson and George I   C. Gerald Ford
4. Sara Delano and James H   D. Richard Nixon
5. Nelle Wilson and John A   E. Lyndon Johnson
6. Jane Randolph and Peter R   F. John Kennedy
7. Susanna Boylston and John S   G. Harry Truman
8. Abigail Smith and John Q   H. Franklin Roosevelt
9. Rose Fitzgerald and Joseph F   I. Warren G. Harding
10. Nancy Allison and William L   J. Woodrow Wilson
11. Martha Young and John G   K. Theodore Roosevelt
12. Hannah Milhous and Frank D   L. William McKinley
13. Lillian Gordy and James B   M. James Garfield
14. Martha Bulloch and Theodore K   N. Rutherford Hayes
15. Jessie Woodrow and Joseph J   O. U. S. Grant
16. Hannah Simpson and Jesse O   P. Abraham Lincoln
17. Sophia Birchard N   Q. John Quincy Adams
    and Rutherford
18. Eliza Ballou and Abram M   R. Thomas Jefferson
19. Nancy Hanks and Thomas P   S. John Adams
20. Rebekah Baines and Samuel E   T. George Washington

111

PRESIDENTIAL CHILDREN QUIZ

Listed below on the left are 20 presidential couples. Twenty of their children are listed on the right. Match the progeny to the parents.

(Score five points for each correct answer.)

1. The Reagans *Q* A. Esther (only child ever born in the White House)

2. The Carters *R* B. Margaret

3. The Fords *G* C. Patsy (child from First Lady's former marriage)

4. The Nixons *L* D. Charles Francis

5. The Johnsons *S* E. John Quincy

6. The Kennedys *M* F. Maria

7. The Eisenhowers *N* G. Susan

8. The Trumans *B* H. Robert

9. The Franklin Roosevelts *T* I. Robert Todd

10. The Coolidges *P* J. Alice

11. The Tafts *H* K. Mary Abigail

12. The Theodore Roosevelts *J* L. Tricia

13. The Clevelands *A* M. John John

14. The Grants *O* N. John

15. The Lincolns *I* O. Nellie

16. The Fillmores *F* P. Calvin, Jr.

17. The John Quincy Adams' *D* Q. Patti

18. The Monroes R. Amy

19. The Adams' *E* S. Linda Bird

20. The Washingtons *C* T. Elliott

The press covers the beginning of the Reagan years.

AMERICAN POLITICAL QUOTATIONS QUIZ

Listed on the left below are 20 political quotations. The men who spoke or wrote them are listed on the right. Match them.

(Score five points for each correct answer.)

1. "It could probably be shown by facts and figures that there is no distinctly native American criminial class except Congress."

   A. H. L. Mencken

2. "We have nothing to fear, but fear itself."

   B. Ulysses S. Grant

3. "I am against government by crony."

   C. Will Durant

4. "The world must be made safe for democracy."

   D. Will Rogers

5. "The only prize much cared for by the powerful is power. The prize of the general is not a bigger tent, but command."

   E. Patrick Henry

6. "Liberty and Union, now and forever, one and inseparable!"

   F. Theodore Roosevelt

7. "As I would not be a slave, so I would not be a master, this expresses my idea of democracy."

   G. Robert G. Ingersoll

8. "When a man assumes a public trust, he should consider himself as public property."

   H. Abraham Lincoln

9. "The responsibility of the great states is to serve and not to dominate the world."

   I. Thomas Jefferson

10. "You shall not press down upon the brow of labor this cross of

    J. Mark Twain

thorns, you shall not crucify
mankind upon a cross of gold!"

11. "Is life so dear, or peace so   K. Daniel Webster
sweet, as to be purchased at the
price of chains and slavery? For-
bid it, almighty God! I know not
what course others may take; but
as for me, give me liberty or give
me death!"

12. "Politics has got so expensive   L. Harold L. Ickes
that it takes a lot of money
to even get beat with."

13. "Like an armed warrior, like   M. Franklin D. Roosevelt
a plumed knight, James G. Blaine
marched down the halls of the
American Congress and threw his
shining lance full and fair
against the brazen forehead of
every traitor to his country and
every maligner of his fair
reputation."

14. "A statesman cannot afford to be N. Harry S. Truman
a moralist."

15. "Leave the matter of religion to   O. William Jennings
the family alter, the church, and   Bryan
the private school, supported
entirely by private contributions.
Keep the church and the state forever separate."

16. "Reformers and professionals are P. Oliver Wendell
like politicians in search of   Holmes, Jr.
jobs; both are trying to bilk the
taxpayers."

17. "The first requisite of a good   Q. Woodrow Wilson
citizen in this country of ours
is that he should be able and
willing to pull his weight."

The U.S. flag and a "Welcome Home Dutch"
celebration is staged as 1976 Republican
presidential candidate Ronald Reagan spoke to a
homecoming rally in the Dixon [Illinois] High
School auditorium.

ANSWERS

ROOTS QUIZ

1. Ireland
2. Potato famine
3. He was an illegal alien.
4. Canada
5. John Edward Reagan
6. Nelle Wilson
7. Scotland and England
8. Catholic
9. Protestant
10. His mother
11. Ray-gan
12. 1911
13. Aquarius
14. Tampico, Illinois
15. Bakery
16. Banking

BOYHOOD QUIZ

1. Dixon
2. Rock River
3. Shoe salesman
4. He was an alcoholic.
5. North High School
6. Train whistles
7. Democratic Party
8. The Birth of a Nation
9. Jewish people
10. True
11. His mother
12. Above average
13. Lifeguard
14. Seven
15. Number of people he saved from drowning
16. Lowell Park
17. Myopia
18. Football, basketball, track
19. Yearbook
20. Yes

YOUNG MANHOOD QUIZ

1. Eureka
2. 220
3. President
4. True
5. Guard
6. Swimming
7. Strike
8. Yes
9. Northwestern
10. Second prize
11. Economics and sociology
12. Chicago
13. Davenport
14. WOC
15. Christmas card
16. Football
17. Five dollars and carfare
18. $100 a month
19. Des Moines
20. Coast to coast

POST-WAR QUIZ

1. Screen Actors Guild
2. Franklin D. Roosevelt
3. Liberal
4. Communist
5. House Committee on Un-American Activities
6. Communist influence in the film industry
7. SAG
8. Six
9. Gun
10. Not that interested

THE NEW DIRECTIONS QUIZ

1. William Holden
2. Mrs. William Holden
3. The Little Brown Church
4. Caesarian
5. Caesarian
6. General Electric
7. 1962
8. Yes
9. Yes. He had been a "Democrat for Eisenhower"
10. "Death Valley Days"
11. Twenty Mule-Team Borax
12. Barry Goldwater
13. William E. Miller
14. Lyndon Baines Johnson
15. Hubert H. Humphrey
16. George Murphy
17. Conservative California businessmen
18. His famous line from Kings Row when he awakes and finds his legs have been amputated.
19. "Death Valley Days" host
20. Edmund G. Brown

GUBERNATORIAL QUIZ I

1. Jack Warner
2. Because of his years in the movies and on TV, he was known by the public.
3. Samuel Yorty
4. An actor
5. Three-to-two
6. Richard M. Nixon
7. Population explosion
8. Yes
9. Russia, West Germany,
10. Bob Hope
11. Sacramento
12. Adolf Hitler
13. If It's Brown, Flush It.
14. 55
15. 61
16. Gene Kelly

117

GUBERNATORIAL QUIZ II

1. Three by five
2. Welfare
3. Almost a million votes
4. 58 percent
5. 1967
6. John Davis Lodge
7. Lew Wallace, author of Ben-Hur
8. Raise taxes
9. State Board of Regents
10. One. The Supreme Court then ruled against the death penalty.
11. He was for the death penalty, believing it to be a deterrent to premeditated murder.
12. Jelly beans
13. Berkeley
14. S. I. Hayakawa
15. 1968
16. Richard Nixon
17. Spiro Agnew
18. Authority
19. 1970
20. January 1971

THE 1976 CONVENTION AND ELECTION QUIZ

1. Red
2. 15
3. Betty
4. Orlando
5. Equal Rights Amendment
6. Richard Schweiker
7. Pennsylvania
8. More liberal
9. Reagan's choice of a man who was somewhat incorrectly perceived as a real liberal hurt Reagan's credibility.
10. Hugh Scott
11. West Virginia
12. Robert Dole
13. Kansas
14. Time magazine (August 30, 1976)
15. Walter Mondale
16. Wisconsin
17. Hubert Humphrey
18. Why Not the Best?
19. Lie to them
20. January 1977

1976 CAMPAIGN QUIZ I

1. Washington, D.C.
2. "Thou shall not speak ill of any other Republican."
3. It was the bicentennial year.
4. New Hampshire
5. He lost.
6. Inflation
7. Whip Inflation Now
8. Spending
9. Henry Kissinger
10. The Panama Canal
11. He won.
12. Gipper
13. An old football helmet
14. All of them
15. In some primaries, Republicans are allowed to vote for Democrats and vice versa.

INTERREGNUM QUIZ

1. His age
2. True
3. Not really
4. He probably would have lost to Carter that year.
5. William Loeb
6. No
7. Yes
8. Ripon
9. Country Clubs and Big Business
10. Citizens for the Republic
11. Phillip Crane
12. Reagan's political right
13. C
14. B
15. D
16. A
17. The Soviet Union
18. George Bush
19. Arm wrestling
20. Connally and Baker

1976 CAMPAIGN QUIZ II

1. Ford
2. 1,130
3. H
4. G
5. C
6. A
7. B
8. F
9. D
10. E
11. 1,505
12. Barry Goldwater
13. John Connally
14. Democrat
15. Kansas City, Missouri
16. The Cow Palace
17. August
18. New York City
19. Madison Square Garden
20. July

RUNS AGAIN QUIZ I

1. New York City
2. New York Hilton Hotel
3. Yes
4. George Bush
5. John Anderson and Phillip Crane
6. John Connally
7. George Bush
8. Howard Baker
9. Bob Dole
10. Telegraph
11. He paid the bill.
12. The stage of the Nashua High School gymnasium
13. John Connally
14. "I'm paying for this microphone, Mr. Green!"
15. John Anderson
16. Howard Baker
17. E
18. Jerry Brown
19. John Anderson
20. Chappaquiddick

RUNS AGAIN QUIZ II

1. More than 50 percent
2. Grand Old Party
3. Bush
4. Kansas
5. John Anderson
6. Vietnam veterans
7. Blacks
8. John Kennedy
9. Kemp-Roth Bill
10. Cuba
11. Economics
12. Bush
13. Howard Baker
14. Beverly Hilton
15. Efram Zimbalist, Jr.
16. E
17. C
18. B
19. A
20. D

THE 1980 REPUBLICAN CONVENTION QUIZ I

1. 1832
2. False. What the Democrats decided did not apply to Republican conventions. Reagan, however, was a shoo-in.
3. Dr. Henry Kissinger
4. Negative
5. True
6. His wife, Betty
7. Herbert Hoover
8. George Bush
9. Detroit
10. July
11. Coleman Young
12. Pat Boone
13. Glen Campbell
14. Billy Graham
15. William Simon
16. Inflation and unemployment
17. Benjamin Hooks
18. Barry Goldwater

THE 1980 REPUBLICAN CONVENTION QUIZ II

1. Henry Kissinger
2. "America for Me"
3. Paul Lazalt
4. Montana
5. John Phillip Sousa
6. Detroit Plaza Hotel
7. Joe Louis Arena
8. Thomas Paine
9. Big Government
10. Franklin D. Roosevelt
11. Jobs
12. The inner cities
13. A TelePrompter
14. Yes
15. A moment of silent prayer
16. "God bless America!"
17. Blue
18. French cuffs

THE 1980 REPUBLICAN CONVENTION QUIZ III

1. 32nd
2. 4,000
3. Bill Brock
4. 2,000
5. 10,000
6. Fire works
7. Transit and sanitation strike
8. Hold their own convention
9. True
10. "Thou shall not be over confident!"
11. John Rhodes
12. Air-conditioning system
13. True
14. "Stop ERA"
15. Theodore Sorensen

THE GEORGE BUSH QUIZ I

1. 13
2. One year
3. Barbara
4. George Herbert Walker Bush
5. Connecticut
6. Banking
7. Andover
8. Yale
9. 1948
10. Publishing
11. Rye
12. Ashley Hall
13. Smith
14. Christmas
15. A dance
16. Houston
17. Oil
18. No
19. House
20. Central Intelligence Agency

THE GEORGE BUSH QUIZ II

1. United Nations
2. China
3. Distinguished Flying Cross
4. Five minutes
5. Style
6. Sunbelt Republicans resent the fact that Bush is part of the "Eastern Establishment," that he went to a prep, school, attended Yale, etc.
7. Trilateral Commission
8. The industrial Northeast
9. William Loeb
10. Foreign policy
11. Reagan's staff
12. False. She didn't particularly like him.
13. True
14. 30 percent tax cut
15. ERA
16. Abortion
17. Eight
18. Pennsylvania
19. Jogged
20. The U.S. Atlantic Fleet

THE JOHN ANDERSON QUIZ

1. The Wailing Wall
2. Menachem Begin
3. Oppose
4. Jerusalem
5. President Anwar Sadat
6. West Berlin
7. Keke
8. Helmut Schmidt
9. Bonn is the capital of West Germany.
10. Valery Giscard d'Estaing
11. Premier
12. Margaret Thatcher
13. 10 Downing Street
14. "Outside the mainstream"
15. Eisenhower
16. Illinois
17. Because Anderson had been very conservative in the past.
18. They are all born-again Christians.
19. True. He later recanted, however.
20. White

THE MORAL MAJORITY QUIZ

1. 30 million
2. 19 percent
3. Reverend Jerry Falwell
4. Lynchburg
5. "Old Time Gospel Hour"
6. Republican platform
7. John Anderson
8. Prohibition Amendment
9. Alaska
10. Prayer
11. Evolution
12. God
13. Ed McAteer
14. Christian Voice
15. Zone
16. True
17. False
18. America
19. National Council of Churches
20. Article VI

THE WOES OF JIMMY CARTER QUIZ

1. B
2. C
3. D
4. A
5. Afghanistan
6. Leonid Brezhenev
7. Bert Lance
8. Libya
9. Andrew Young
10. Ronald Reagan
11. "I'll admit to being irresponsible if he'll admit to being responsible."
12. David Rockefeller and Henry Kissinger
13. November 4, 1979
14. Those released were either female or black.
15. The Shah
16. Panama
17. Egypt
18. Eight
19. Edmund Muskie
20. 52

THE CARTER/REAGAN DEBATE QUIZ

1. Tuesday, October 28, 1980
2. Cleveland
3. The League of Women Voters
4. Howard K. Smith
5. Barbara Walters
6. 90 minutes
7. Shaking hands
8. Reagan
9. Carter
10. Carter
11. Carter
12. Reagan
13. Carter
14. Carter
15. Reagan
16. Reagan
17. B
18. C
19. A
20. Yes, the debate apparently convinced the American people that Reagan was a reasonable man.

THE 1980 ELECTION QUIZ I

1. True
2. 51 percent Reagan; 41 percent Carter
3. 43,267,489
4. 34,964,583
5. 5,588,014
6. 270
7. 489
8. 49
9. Seven percent
10. Six
11. 44
12. Minnesota
13. Hawaii
14. His home state, Georgia
15. West Virginia
16. Maryland
17. Rhode Island
18. The South
19. The State of Israel
20. True

THE 1980 ELECTION QUIZ II

1. Inflation
2. A breakthrough in the hostage situation
3. No
4. Independent voters
5. War
6. 47 percent
7. 26 years
8. 12
9. 33
10. Four
11. Debate between Carter and Reagan
12. "Are you happier today than when Mr. Carter became president?"
13. 9:45 PM
14. The West Coast
15. 1888
16. Senator Kennedy
17. Century Plaza Hotel
18. The United States of 9.33America
19. The states that Reagan carried in the electoral college.
20. The Stock Market

ELECTORAL VOTE QUIZ

1.	Q	11.	E
2.	P	12.	A
3.	R	13.	B
4.	L	14.	I
5.	O	15.	F
6.	N	16.	J
7.	M	17.	C
8.	D	18.	K
9.	H	19.	Rhode Island
10.	G	20.	Three

THE "WHO VOTED FOR RONALD REAGAN?" QUIZ

1.	B	11.	M
2.	C	12.	K
3.	A	13.	L
4.	F	14.	O
5.	D	15.	N
6.	E	16.	P
7.	H	17.	S
8.	G	18.	Q
9.	J	19.	T
10.	I	20.	R

THE SENATE RACE QUIZ I

1.	97th	9.	Cranston
2.	53	10.	Hart
3.	46	11.	Dodd
4.	None	12.	Hawkins
5.	Denton	13.	Mattingly
6.	Murkowski	14.	Inouye
7.	Goldwater	15.	Symms
8.	Bumpers	16.	Dixon

THE SENATE RACE QUIZ II

1. Long
2. Mathias
3. Eagleton
4. Laxalt
5. Rudman
6. D'Amato
7. East
8. Andrews
9. Glenn
10. Nickles
11. Packwood
12. Spector
13. Hollings
14. Abdnor
15. Garn
16. Leahy
17. Gorton

THE BREAKUP OF THE DEMOCRATIC COALITION QUIZ

1. 1953-1961
2. The social issue
3. True
4. The family
5. The South
6. Population
7. Chicago in 1968
8. Daley
9. True
10. Hubert Humphrey
11. Edmund Muskie
12. Thomas Eagleton
13. Missouri
14. Sargent Shriver
15. Spiro Agnew
16. Kevin Phillips
17. Watergate
18. Inflation
19. Equal Rights Amenament
20. Ted Sorensen

THE REAGAN-STYLE QUIZ

1. Red
2. Adolfo
3. Bill Blass and Albert Nippon
4. Cigars
5. Off-color
6. Aida Grey
7. Bloomingdale
8. Alfred Bloomingdale
9. Frank Sinatra
10. Dean Martin
11. He loves it!
12. Jimmy Stewart
13. Elizabeth Taylor
14. Ponita Granville
15. True
16. Underdone
17. Eggplant lasagne
18. Macaroni and cheese
19. Brownies
20. "Insult me!"

NANCY, OUR NEW FIRST LADY QUIZ I

1. First Lady
2. Nancy
3. 1923
4. Anne Francis Robbins
5. Car salesman
6. Nancy
7. Actress
8. Edith "Deedee" Luckett
9. Her father left her mother.
10. Two
11. Loyal Davis
12. Neurosurgeon
13. Chicago
14. 14
15. 16
16. Casino Club
17. Girls' Latin School
18. To be an actress
19. Smith

NANCY, OUR FIRST LADY QUIZ II

1. Drug
2. Mentally retarded
3. She's against them.
4. Liquor
5. California
6. Red
7. Vodka
8. Spencer Tracy
9. MGM
10. 1949

THE REAGAN FAMILY QUIZ I

1. Two years younger
2. California
3. Advertising executive
4. Four
5. Michael Edward Reagan
6. Twice
7. Agricultural Energy Resources
8. Maureen Elizabeth Reagan
9. Twice
10. Yes

THE REAGAN FAMILY QUIZ II

1. Patricia Reagan
2. Patricia Davis
3. Lived with him
4. Bernie Leadon
5. Los Angeles, California
6. They are all college drop-outs.
7. Cameron Reagan
8. Colleen
9. Santa Barbara
10. Horseback ride
11. Pacific Palisades
12. Antique
13. His father was an alcoholic.
14. Ronald Prescott
15. To Michael
16. Michael was getting marrried.
17. Helen Gurley Brown of Cosmopolitan
18. His privacy
19. 588 to 650 acres (reports vary)
20. His wife, Nancy, is far closer to him than anyone else in the world.

RONALD PRESCOTT REAGAN'S MARRIAGE QUIZ

1. Doria Felissa Palmieri
2. A year and a half
3. New York
4. She's a literary researcher
5. Civil
6. 29
7. Secret Service agent
8. Small gold band
9. No
10. No
11. Ronald Prescott
12. Doria
13. True
14. Champagne
15. Stanley Holden

THE BROOKE ASTOR PARTY QUIZ I

1. Park Avenue
2. The Astor Foundation
3. George Will
4. Yes
5. No
6. E
7. C
8. A
9. D
10. B

THE BROOKE ASTOR PARTY QUIZ II

1. No
2. Yes
3. No
4. No
5. Happy Rockefeller
6. Tom Brokaw
7. John Chancellor
8. Yes
9. Five
10. Tito
11. Westchester
12. No
13. Tiffany's
14. Yes
15. The latter
16. New York City

THE QUINTESSENTIAL REAGAN QUIZ

1. Six feet, one inch
2. 185
3. Blue
4. Although we wouldn't bet our lives on it, apparently he does not!
5. Grey and brown (or chestnut)
6. White
7. Solid-color
8. A white handkerchief
9. Western garb
10. Little Man is President Reagan's beautiful thoroughbred stallion.
11. Yes
12. His heart
13. A hard-luck story
14. When he reads and/or writes
15. Hay Fever
16. Prostate
17. Yes
18. Jack Kemp
19. The latter
20. Land

PRESIDENT REAGAN'S CABINET QUIZ

1. Alexander Haig
2. Richard Nixon's
3. Casper Willard Weinberger
4. Book reviews
5. War Department
6. William French Smith
7. Donald T. Regan
8. Samuel Pierce
9. Housing and Urban Development
10. Richard Shultz Schweiker
11. Malcolm Baldrige
12. Ray Donovan
13. Andrew Lindsay Lewis, Jr.
14. John Block
15. James G. Watt
16. James B. Edwards
17. Terrel H. Bell
18. William Casey
19. Central Intelligence Agency
20. David Stockman

THE NATION'S CAPITAL QUIZ I

1. District of Columbia
2. Maryland and Virginia
3. Potomac
4. Less
5. Washington Post
6. George Washington
7. The Capitol
8. Philadelphia
9. Thomas Jefferson
10. 1814
11. 1600 Pennsylvania
12. Arlington National Cemetery
13. Executive (President and Cabinet), Legislative (Congress) and Judicial (Supreme Court)
14. The Capitol
15. Congress
16. The Senate and the House of Representatives
17. The Library of Congress
18. The National Archives
19. Georgetown
20. Washington Redskins

THE NATION'S CAPITAL QUIZ II

1. False. A subway was opened in 1976.
2. Lincoln and Jefferson
3. God
4. Washington
5. 1961
6. The Folger Shakespeare Memorial Library
7. The National Art Gallery
8. Walter Reed Hospital
9. Mount Vernon
10. Robert Taft
11. Pentagon
12. The Smithsonian
13. Arlington Memorial Bridge
14. Cherry trees
15. Saint Peter and Saint Paul
16. Saint Paul
17. George Washington University
18. Economics and the social sciences
19. The Civil War
20. Winston Churchill

THE FIRST LADIES QUIZ I

1. E	11. Q
2. P	12. L
3. D	13. R
4. G	14. S
5. H	15. I
6. C	16. K
7. F	17. J
8. N	18. A
9. B	19. T
10. M	20. O

MIDDLE NAMES OF THE U.S. PRESIDENTS QUIZ

1. I	11. L
2. O	12. F
3. G	13. I
4. H	14. S
5. K	15. T
6. B	16. R
7. M	17. P
8. D	18. Q
9. A	19. E
10. N	20. C

THE FIRST LADIES QUIZ II

1. O	9. L
2. D	10. H
3. F	11. K
4. E	12. J
5. G	13. M
6. B	14. N
7. A	15. I
8. C	

THE SUPREME COURT QUIZ

1. William Howard Taft
2. Thurgood Marshall

3. False	12. J
4. No	13. C
5. F.D.R.	14. L
6. N	15. M
7. E	16. K
8. D	17. F
9. G	18. A
10. I	19. B
11. O	20. H

THE PRESIDENTIAL QUIZ I

1. J	11. D
2. R	12. F
3. L	13. G
4. M	14. T
5. I	15. A
6. S	16. Q
7. N	17. K
8. C	18. B
9. E	19. P
10. H	20. O

THE PRESIDENTIAL QUIZ II

1. K	11. H
2. I or J	12. D
3. Q	13. B
4. I or J	14. L
5. R	15. S
6. F	16. M
7. P	17. A
8. C	18. E
9. G	19. O
10. T	20. N

THE VICE PRESIDENTIAL QUIZ I

1. C	11. O
2. P	12. N
3. G	13. F
4. H	14. E
5. I	15. A
6. Q	16. A
7. K	17. B
8. J	
9. L	
10. M	

THE VICE PRESIDENTIAL QUIZ II

1.	S or T	11.	M
2.	E	12.	B, C or D
3.	S or T	13.	B, C or D
4.	K or L	14.	B, C or D
5.	K or L	15.	U
6.	A	16.	J
7.	F	17.	I
8.	R	18.	G
9.	Q	19.	N or O
10.	P	20.	N or O

THE STATES OF THE PRESIDENTS QUIZ I

1.	A	11.	E
2.	B	12.	A
3.	A	13.	D
4.	A	14.	F
5.	A	15.	G
6.	B	16.	H
7.	C	17.	E
8.	D	18.	I
9.	A	19.	I
10.	A	20.	I

THE STATES OF THE PRESIDENTS QUIZ II

1.	A	11.	F
2.	B	12.	D
3.	C	13.	G
4.	B	14.	L
5.	C	15.	M
6.	B	16.	L
7.	C	17.	K
8.	D	18.	J
9.	C	19.	I
10.	A	20.	H

ELECTORAL STATES' NICKNAMES QUIZ I

1.	I	11.	B
2.	K	12.	G
3.	J	13.	E
4.	O	14.	L
5.	P	15.	R
6.	C	16.	T
7.	M	17.	S
8.	D	18.	Q
9.	F	19.	A
10.	H	20.	N

ELECTORAL STATES' NICKNAMES QUIZ II

1.	J	11.	H
2.	I	12.	N
3.	G	13.	F
4.	M	14.	E
5.	O	15.	D
6.	P	16.	Q
7.	S	17.	C
8.	K	18.	L
9.	B	19.	R
10.	T	20.	A

ELECTORAL STATES' CAPITALS QUIZ I

1.	H	11.	M
2.	J	12.	K
3.	L	13.	I
4.	N	14.	C
5.	O	15.	G
6.	P	16.	F
7.	T	17.	E
8.	S	18.	D
9.	R	19.	A
10.	Q	20.	B

ELECTORAL STATES' CAPITALS QUIZ II

1.	F	11.	I
2.	G	12.	H
3.	J	13.	E
4.	K	14.	R
5.	L	15.	T
6.	N	16.	Q
7.	S	17.	C
8.	M	18.	D
9.	O	19.	A
10.	P	20.	B

U.S. HISTORY QUIZ I

1.	S	11.	R
2.	F	12.	T
3.	G	13.	E
4.	H	14.	C
5.	A	15.	Q
6.	B	16.	D
7.	L	17.	P
8.	K	18.	M
9.	J	19.	N
10.	O	20.	I

U.S. HISTORY QUIZ II

1.	K	11.	J
2.	T	12.	N
3.	S	13.	I
4.	D	14.	F
5.	F	15.	E
6.	M	16.	C
7.	Q	17.	B
8.	O	18.	L
9.	R	19.	P
10.	G	20.	A

THE FIRST REPUBLICAN PRESIDENT QUIZ

1. It was there that he got his start in politics. He is also buried there.
2. Kentucky
3. February 12, 1809
4. Thomas
5. Nancy Hanks
6. Springfield
7. Law
8. No
9. Representative in Congress
10. U.S. Senator
11. Stephen A. Douglas
12. Ann Todd
13. 1860
14. True
15. 1861 to 1865
16. 1863
17. John Wilkes Booth
18. Ford's Theatre
19. Our Country Cousin
20. Edwin Stanton

AMERICAN POLITICAL PARTIES QUIZ

1. Elephant
2. Donkey
3. Abraham Lincoln in 1860
4. Andrew Jackson in 1828
5. Federalist
6. Democratic-Republican
7. Whig
8. Greenback
9. Democratic
10. Socialist
11. Democrat Alfred Smith in 1928
12. States' Rights
13. Henry Wallace
14. Republican
15. Democrat Woodrow Wilson
16. Bull Moose
17. Teapot Dome
18. Socialist
19. Curtis LeMay
20. Democratic

PRESIDENTIAL LOSERS QUIZ

1. C
2. E
3. D
4. G
5. F
6. S
7. R
8. B
9. Q
10. P
11. H
12. O
13. L
14. M
15. N
16. K
17. J
18. T
19. A
20. I

PRESIDENTIAL OCCUPATIONS QUIZ

1. D
2. E
3. G
4. H
5. I
6. M
7. K
8. L
9. N
10. O
11. P
12. C
13. A
14. Q
15. R
16. B
17. S
18. T
19. F
20. J

PRESIDENTIAL RELIGION QUIZ

1. Episcopalian
2. Presbyterian
3. Baptist
4. Episcopalian
5. Disciples of Christ
6. Theodore Roosevelt
7. Episcopalian
8. False. He had no formal religious affiliation.
9. True
10. Methodist
11. I
12. D
13. G
14. C
15. B
16. A
17. J
18. H
19. F
20. E

THE PRESIDENTIAL POTPOURRI QUIZ I

1. Woodrow Wilson
2. Theodore and Franklin Roosevelt
3. Franklin D. Roosevelt
4. Dwight D. Eisenhower
5. John F. Kennedy
6. Grover Cleveland
7. Andrew Johnson
8. James Garfield and William McKinley
9. Charles J. Guiteau shot Garfield. Leon Czolgosz shot McKinley.
10. Lee Harvey Oswald
11. Jack Ruby
12. Sirhan Sirhan
13. William Howard Taft, 280 pounds
14. Abe Lincoln, six-feet-four
15. Andrew Jackson
16. Ronald Reagan
17. Chester A. Arthur, Woodrow Wilson and Grover Cleveland
18. Abraham Lincoln
19. Theodore Roosevelt and Woodrow Wilson
20. Thomas Jefferson

THE PRESIDENTIAL POTPOURRI QUIZ II

1. Teddy Roosevelt was 42.
2. Jack Kennedy was 43.
3. Ronald Reagan was 69.
4. William Henry Harrison was 68.
5. John Adams
6. Herbert Hoover
7. 88
8. 79
9. Millard Fillmore, James Buchanan and James Garfield
10. Andrew Jackson
11. John Adams and Thomas Jefferson
12. Thomas Jefferson
13. John Tyler
14. Zachary Taylor
15. Andrew Jackson
16. James Buchanan and Grover Cleveland
17. Pneumonia
18. John Adams and John Quincy Adams
19. William Henry Harrison and Benjamin Harrison
20. Theodore Roosevelt

COLLEGES OF THE PRESIDENTS QUIZ

1. N	11. G
2. P	12. H
3. T	13. I
4. Q	14. F
5. S	15. J
6. K	16. E
7. O	17. A
8. C	18. M
9. R	19. L
10. D	20. B

PARENTS OF THE PRESIDENTS QUIZ

1. T	11. G
2. C	12. D
3. I	13. B
4. H	14. K
5. A	15. J
6. R	16. O
7. S	17. N
8. Q	18. M
9. F	19. P
10. L	20. E

PRESIDENTIAL CHILDREN QUIZ

1. Q	11. H
2. R	12. J
3. G	13. A
4. L	14. O
5. S	15. I
6. M	16. K
7. N	17. D
8. B	18. F
9. T	19. E
10. P	20. C

AMERICAN POLITICAL QUOTATIONS QUIZ

1. J	10. O
2. M	11. E
3. L	12. D
4. Q	13. G
5. P	14. C
6. K	15. B
7. H	16. A
8. I	17. F
9. N	